Living a Dog's Life

Jazzy, Juicy, and Me

ALSO BY CINDY ADAMS

The Gift of Jazzy

ST. MARTIN'S PRESS
NEW YORK

Living a Dog's Life

Jazzy, Juicy, and Me

CINDY ADAMS

To my mom, who would have loved my
Jazzy and Juicy

Contents

Living a Dog's Life

Jazzy, Juicy, and Me

ONE

The Devils

 It's nighttime that the Devils dance. It's when the surrounding universe is dead that the dark world within comes alive.

When sleep is a stranger is when Fear's fingers grab hold. It's then that the Voices shout:

"You're all alone."

"Nobody really cares."

"Suppose you fall . . . suppose you get sick . . ."

"If anything happens, who would know?"

"How long before someone might find you?"

Punch the pillow, smooth the sheets, roll over on your side. The Voices get louder:

"Who would you call?"

"Who would rush over?"

"Who would care?"

"Everybody has somebody, you have nobody."

Switch on the light, open a book, raid the fridge, switch off the light, crawl back in bed. The Voices:

"You're getting older."

"You need someone with you."

"You shouldn't be alone."

"What if . . ."

The What Ifs subdivide. What If there's a fire? What If an earthquake? What If a terrorist attack? What If you can't breathe?

The first feathers of dawn usher in the army of Yeah Buts. Yeah But I don't want someone cluttering up my space anymore. Yeah But I love my life as it is. Yeah But I've been there, done that, and don't want to be married again.

The What Ifs wade in. What If it isn't a full-time commitment? What If you don't marry him? What If you just have someone live with you?

I opened a dialogue with the Devils: "Look, I was married a lifetime. He was good to me and I loved him, but I've paid my dues. For his last ten years I took care of a husband who'd grown old and who was dying. I'm not doing that a second time."

"So find a husband who's grown old and who's healthy," said the Devils.

"Yeah? A geezer with his three hairs parted right over the ears and pasted across a bare skull sideways? A beauty with denture breath? For Christmas you buy him an economy-size jar of Polident? No, not for me."

I've seen these types sitting on benches in Miami. In green-checked polyester pants. Their futures behind them. To them exercise is a brisk sit. Late dinner is the early bird special at six o'clock. Farina is an exotic food.

I told the Devils: "You're talking men whose social calendar is two prostate exams a week. And their conversation? 'You heard how cold it is up north?'"

Unfortunately, even if the Devils hadn't already whispered that I wasn't exactly Reese Witherspoon and wasn't exactly about to find Justin Timberlake hitting on me, I didn't want a young stud either.

Tragically, I'd actually seen myself in a five-times magnifying mirror. In broad daylight. In summer. Right next to a window. With bright sun beating down. Trust me, this was not a good thing. I wanted to go under the wheels of a speeding truck.

My chin resembled Sherwood Forest. There was more hair on my face than there was on my head. I didn't need a tweezer. I needed a scythe.

A friend asked me the other day: "You know what I think is the world's best invention?"

I took a guess: "Radar?"

"No."

"TV?"

"No."

"Cell phone?"

"No."

"A spaceship?"

"Thong panties."

Thong panties?! I mean, whatever happened to radium, contact lenses, polio vaccine? Thong panties?! Okay, depilatories I can understand. Thong panties?!

I stared at her. She wasn't much better looking than I. How come she was finding a need for thong panties and I wasn't? I wondered, How come I've obviously missed out on so much that I've never even had the need for thong panties? The once I tried them, they ended up bunched in my crack.

When I shop for underpants, I go looking for size fours. Five is nice. Six feels so comfortable. I buy sevens.

It's not that I don't manage to look glamorous. I dress to the eyeballs when I'm out. Take a particular fund-raiser for Andrew Cuomo. At the time he was political royalty. He had been in Bill Clinton's cabinet. He's the son of New York's onetime governor Mario Cuomo. He's the ex-husband of Robert Kennedy's daughter Kerry Kennedy. He's the brother-in-law of fashion star Kenneth Cole and the brother of TV journalist Chris Cuomo. So this particular night it was a big-time crowd whooping up Andrew's New York gubernatorial try.

Emcee Rosie O'Donnell stood on the stage of the jammed Sheraton Grand Ballroom. Despite one thousand VIPs, Rosie wore her usual fashion-forward sweats, sneakers, and crappy baseball jacket. She spotted me sitting with our long-ago governor Mario Cuomo and our state's former First Lady Matilda Cuomo. Across a football-size room she shouted: "And there's Cindy Adams. Overdressed as usual."

I shouted back: "And you look like an unmade bed."

Rosie and I have long had this running gag. I tell her she's the poster girl for a bundle of wet wash. She tells me my birth certificate must've been written on a bugle bead. The truth is, I was all tarted up. But that was out in public. At home my ensembles are straight from Rosie's closet, and I'm the visual equivalent of five miles of bad road. So I knew I couldn't deal with a young guy. Suddenly having to always look good? Smell good? Shave my legs every day? Drizzling fragrance once more on those seven desirable spots which these days I only use about four of?

On freezing February nights I'd have to opt for frilly, frothy, froufrou nighties instead of flannels with the trapdoor and feet in them. Naaaahhh, I thought, I really don't want to do that. And let's don't even discuss the bikini wax.

The Devils were making so much noise in my head that I couldn't get a fix on that still small voice of gratitude I try to chat with in the quiet hours. Many's the night I invite that friendly familiar whisper to keep me company. Sometimes It comes in so faintly that you can barely hear It, but It always comes. This time nothing came through, but I knew what It would have said had the static not been so loud.

It would have told me to be grateful, to count my blessings, to realize how fortunate I was. And It would have been right. It knew. And I knew. I knew no fairy godmother had touched me with a magic wand. I wasn't born with breathtaking beauty, blue-blood upbringing, or a silver spoon. My parents never gave me an eighteen-karat-gold Rolex. I didn't go to college. I wasn't left a fortune. Money was not something my family had in profusion. My divorced single-parent mother, whom I adored, was an executive secretary; the kindly gentleman she married down the line who became my dad for much of my life was an insurance man. I was a sickly baby. When Mom got divorced she pawned things and we moved in with her mother.

Grandma was a janitress. Grandma came from the old country with a handful of children she fed by cleaning the stoops of brownstones. And by taking in boarders. Life with Grandma was simple. Whatever was dirty got scrubbed in the kitchen sink. Mom finally saved enough for a party dress for me. It was satin with shreds of kolinsky fur. Grandma washed it. With brown laundry soap. And put it on a steam pipe to dry. It went stiff.

My public school classmates were picture postcard pretty. Jeanette with waist-length blond hair, Joanne with silken braids, Suzanne with thick auburn curls. I had acne, anemia, and my looks weren't A-1. Good teeth I had. The only thing I didn't need was dentistry. Since my birth father was a dentist, I always thought that was somehow a waste. But in Mom's eyes I was beautiful. She even took me to a modeling agency. I stood there in my blue-and-yellow-plaid wool jumper and yellow sweater, and they politely looked me over. Then they politely refused me.

"She's heavy," they said.

"She is *not* heavy," mother said. "She is just short for her weight."

The weight was shifting from foot to foot as I stood in the middle of the room.

"My daughter *will* become something," my mother said.

"We're sure she will," they said. "But not here."

My mother, who was beautiful, determined to make me attractive. She had my hairline moved back, and when she realized my nose was in the image and likeness of the dentist she'd divorced because she hadn't liked any part of him, including his nose, she brought me to a friend's relative. He was a plastic surgeon. His surgery was off his kitchen. Fact is, it *was* his kitchen. In Brooklyn yet.

Mom then had me audition for some small-time creep theatrical agent with a smelly cigar and a walk-up hole-in-the-wall rear office in a seedy building in the Theater District because he "guaranteed" he'd make me a movie star. What did we know? We were so eager, so unsavvy. The problem was, he wanted a certain amount of money each week for his coaching. We didn't have it, which is the reason I never became a movie star.

In school I had a 99 average and was in the rapid advancement class, but we had to make our graduation dresses. By midsemester my white lawn had osmosed into black serge, and the dress I was mangling might've fit Quasimodo but me—never. I just couldn't do it. The teacher announced I wouldn't get my diploma if I didn't sew my graduation outfit. My mother told her, "My kid is never going to have to make her own clothes," and marched me out of school. Age fifteen marked the end of my formal education and the beginning of my modeling career.

The one beauty title that repeats and repeats in my ear was when the board of the Better Bagel Bakers Association voted me Miss Bagel. A crown of shellacked bagels was placed upon my then blond head, an auspicious beginning for Miss Cindy Heller's slow, tortuous journey to immortality.

So, although luck is the end product of backbreaking hard work, I know I'm lucky. Am I grateful for my lifestyle, the boldface names that are now my friends, and the high-profile job I have as a gossip columnist six days a week for the *New York Post?* Yes. Yes. Of course, yes. But does that make me any the less needy for another heart to lean my head on? No. Whether dinner is on Ming tables or upended cartons, those demons . . . they can be scary.

———

The Voices had become so loud they were shouting. I argued them down. I told them: "Look, I don't need anyone young or old. I have Jazzy." Jazzy is the star of my very own shaggy love story. Jazzy. My seven-pound, purebred, spoiled rotten Yorkshire terrier. My love, my bedmate. Jazzy snuggles under my arm. Jazzy curls between my legs. Jazzy makes his bed right on my chest. No matter how I trained any two-legged household pet, he couldn't give me what Jazzy does. Animals meet the expectations of the heart. I don't love Jazzy. I am *in* love with him. No, I thought, I don't really need anything or anyone else. I have Jazzy.

And then came Verizon.

Came the day my phones went out. Not even wrong numbers got through. Not even heavy breathers or bill collectors. For three weeks my phone lay as dead in its bed as Princess Diana used to say Charles was.

On a cell with the battery running down, I rang whatever the phone company was that week—AT&T, Lucent, Avaya, Bell South, Bell North, Bell Up Yours, Verizon, Sprint, Screw, Whatever—and then held on. That's what you do when you call "emergency service." You hold on—until the emergency and, you hope, they—are long over. This is a communications operation, but there is no such thing as communicating with them. The last human voice associated with this operation was the one who presided over AT&T's breakup.

You get a menu. Press 1 if your bill is incorrect, press 2 if your payment will be delayed, press 3 if because of this you're going to be late to work. When you cannot reach this emergency service, how are they going to perform said emergency service? Where? On what? What's Verizon's idea of emergency service? Putting a tourniquet on a hit-and-run victim's cell phone?

The history of this giant is "Tell." Telephone, telecommunications, television, teletype, telex, tell-a-friend. But tell *them*? Forget it.

My assistant, Marcee, who has worked for me for a lifetime and who's so able she could get Osama bin Laden and Saddam Hussein on a conference call, rousted out a supervisor. The supervisor guaranteed service the next day. For three weeks, because a skyscraper was being built on my corner and in the dredging a lineman had accidentally drilled through a cable, I had no telephones. Also no TV. An elevator man in my Park Avenue building told me: "I live in the projects. In the Bronx. I pay four fifty a month. I have telephones and television."

One particular starless night I was terrified. Not even a spirit could get through to me on a Ouija board, and from constant usage the batteries on my two cells had gone down. The TV was dead, my faxes were dead. The house was eerily quiet. I wasn't feeling comfortable. Our apartment building has a regular outside landline, but there was no communicating with downstairs. The entire building was out. The doorman had no working line either.

I ran into the kitchen and jiggled the house phone. Whatever had hacked through the cables had taken that out, too. The house phone was dead.

I panicked. Nobody could communicate with me nor I with them. At this moment nobody anywhere would know if I was even alive. I was high in the sky in a silent penthouse all alone. Not one soul knew my whereabouts. Nobody to whom I could reach out.

It was terrifying. I calmed myself and thought, I'm okay. I'll be okay. I'll go downstairs to the street. I'll ring one of my friends.

I quickly threw on some clothes, grabbed Jazzy, put his leash on him, and ran out to the little vestibule that fronts my apartment. I rang the elevator bell. No response. I rang again. Nothing. I kept ringing. I shouted. I banged on the service elevator. It didn't respond. It, too, was dead.

My heart was beating fast, and I felt an icy stab of terror. I was totally isolated. Cut off from everything. Completely on my own.

The Voices were winning. The Devils had filled up my dance card.

And then . . . the phone rang.

Service had been restored.

Reacting to this sudden sound, Jazzy wobbled around crazily. At the first ring he began to bark. At the second ring he licked my eyelids and happily powered up that two-inch tail. It was as though the only blood relative I have to call my own was telling me: "Hey . . . it's okay. What were you getting so worked up about? Life's great . . . we're fine . . . let's move on."

TWO

Two Barks Are Better Than One

 Slowly, very slowly, it was the canine version of the dawning of Aquarius. Slowly, very slowly, it began to dawn on me that maybe, just maybe, I should consider the disloyal possibility of . . . just only maybe . . . parenting another dog. I couldn't believe that I'd even dare open the door to such strange thoughts, let alone entertain them. I felt like a traitor.

Jazzy wasn't a dog. He wasn't an animal. He was that warm body I rolled onto when I opened my eyes every morning. The one who shared my mattress. The one I kissed good night. He was the male in my life. The prime live-in of my household. Jazzy Adams couldn't have been more a partner to me if he was splitting the expenses.

Slowly, very slowly, as I ruminated on how attached we were, I stole sideways glances at this creature who, at this particular isolated moment of my ruminations, was parked at my foot happily nibbling my right big toe.

Mother and son gazed at one another. Such love. His big brown eyes so sweet and innocent. He put his head up for petting. I petted it. He waggled away contentedly. I couldn't have loved him more if a doctor had wrenched him out of my own womb. I started beating myself up. Was I thinking such alien hostile thoughts as taking in another dog because I was selfish? Worried what would happen to me if something happened to him? Or was I into this mode because I was selfless? Concerned because I basically knew it was best for him not to be an only dog?

In the middle of my mental argument, a car alarm in the street went off. Jazzy therefore went off. For some reason known only to him and maybe a canine psychologist, he dove under the bed's dust ruffle. To my surprise, once there he relocated his long-lost delicacy. The Greenie is some chlorophyll bone-shaped green thing that's sold in pet shops. What this actually is, God knows. What this actually does, I know. It turns Jazzy into the Antichrist. Try to wrench it away from him and your heretofore docile sweet loving pet becomes the Lion King.

Unlike Jazzy, I was not into Greenies. I somehow couldn't connect with anything black or white either. I was into gray. Unsettled because I sometimes had to leave my beloved alone for a few hours when it couldn't be helped. I was a working person, so occasionally he was a latchkey pet, sitting home alone, waiting. Because I loved him so desperately and because I needed him to have a full rich happy life, I began to consider the possibility that maybe . . . just maybe . . . Jazzy should have a companion.

That didn't mean bonding with another human, like a dog walker or trainer. He needed his own kind.

There was also that small frisson of anxiety that someday somehow something somewhere could happen to him someplace. And there was the accompanying panic that I didn't think I could survive it. As to whether I was more concerned for Jazzy or for myself . . . it's a crapshoot.

I only know it was barely a week before, on Halloween night, that I'd become aware of how dominant a personality he was in my life. I'd spent Halloween with Vanessa, a beautiful young Venezuelan-born socialite whose expertise is political science and Mick Jagger. She's majored in both. We are friends although our lifestyles do not mesh. She first goes out at 11:00 P.M., which is when I'm dragging myself home. Halloween she took me to Bungalow 8, the season's hot spot. By midnight, about when types like Liv Tyler and Leonardo DiCaprio arrive, my ears and lungs had stopped working from the noise and lack of air, so I was on my way home. I stripped off my sequin mask and multicolored wig. Next came the costume. I was just starting to undress when I caught sight of Mr. Jazzy lolling on my bedspread. He was watching me intently. What can I tell you? I actually ducked behind a screen before I peeled off the bra and panties.

Because he didn't have to share anything with anyone,

Jazzy was wildly spoiled. We're talking attitude up the kazoo. We were both thirsty? I went to the tap, he got bottled water. We both had a conflicting appointment, such as the snowy night I had a six o'clock opening and he had a six o'clock playdate with a Westie across town and neither of us could get anywhere without wheels? Jazzy got them. I stayed home. I complained to Reggie, my driver of thirty years: "Reggie, I need you." His answer? "Yeah, but Jazzy needs me first."

I was already crazed because Jazzy had lost a small patch of hair on his left side. He hadn't been bitten by anything. Wasn't scratching in that spot. Hadn't come into contact with any underbrush. I mean, there's not a lot of underbrush in my apartment even on the days my housekeeper, Nazalene, who's been with me nine years, takes off. Although he'd lost fewer hairs than Bruce Willis has left, I was insanely busy bathing him in lotions and checking for allergies and administering vegetable oil and checking his diet. I'd been advised to feed him a little pill. I stuck the tiny pill in a pinkieful of ice cream, and he dutifully took it. "Good boy," I said. I then turned my back. Good boy spit it out.

I was madly busy ministering to him. While he was definitely surviving the hair situation, it was becoming obvious that he might not survive *me*! Friends told me I really had to annex a second family member.

It was suggested I get a cat. This was not for me. Dogs have masters, cats have staff. Jazzy needed another warm body who talked his own language, and I figured I should concentrate on a girl companion. Too much competition if I brought in another boy. The books all tell you for the original pet to remain the alpha dog, the new addition should be smaller. Younger.

Thinking of a sister or brother for Jazzy made me think of his real siblings. To start conditioning him, I first had a visit with Jazzy's biological sister Ahava, who lives with a Connecticut couple. I wanted to see if Jazzy could grow less possessive and jealous if he was sharing with another creature of his own flesh and blood, one who actually came out of the same litter.

No. This prizewinner of mine couldn't have cared less. It was me who ended up on the floor doing the playing. It was me who was crawling around on all fours retrieving the toys. I all but ate his Alpo. The one of us who bonded most with Ahava was me.

Paula Segnatelli of Barnhill Kennels in Woodbury, Connecticut, a breeder of champion Yorkies, had brought both these creatures into the world, and that particular week she'd brought six more pups into the world.

I'd never seen pups just days old. The eyes weren't open, the ears were folded over. They were all-over dark. Each was about four ounces. The size of a mouse. Paula cupped my hands together and placed one in my palm. I couldn't stroke it except by flexing my thumbs. But I couldn't take my eyes off it. These, too, were of the same lineage as Jazzy. Different mother, same macho he-man papa.

Yorkies are like peanuts. You can't stop at just one. I

wanted the whole lot, but that was impossible. I couldn't exactly turn my home into a kennel, and besides, I wouldn't know how to handle them. I couldn't even handle Jazzy.

I tucked one little baby under my shirt, right on my heart. Jazzy, who must've been a CIA agent in another life, was watching. He never took his eyes off me. If a Yorkshire terrier's eyes could become slits, this one's did. I put the little baby, still protectively cupped in my two hands, under Jazzy's nose so he'd catch the scent.

"This is your relative. Your kin. Your third cousin four times removed or whatever," I said.

Boy, was this not love at first sight. My sweet lovable cuddly darling beloved let out a low growl. It was visceral. It came from inside his gizzard somewhere.

He stood there. Growling. I eventually tried pulling him away. He wouldn't move. I tugged at him so hard that the floor had skid marks.

And then, in pattered a tiny teacup Paula had been keeping for her own. "This teeny thing's too little. This one's a mistake. I love her. I can't give her away," said Paula.

She had a face like a cat. Flat shiny patent leather nose the size of a period. Big whiskers. Large eyes set wide apart. Yorkies do most of their growing in their first months. This one was ten months old, two pounds, two ounces and not going to get larger.

"This one will hold her own with anything," Paula told me.

This one was so eentsy that she walked *under* other small dogs.

This one was not to be denied. It was either her way or the highway. She had no idea she was little. She was the size of my compact, yet it was as if she'd been raised in the barrios of Brooklyn and had to fight to make the Big Time. A no-nonsense diva, she fixed you unwaveringly with those big eyes and addressed each approach with an intent "I'm here!" attitude. She badgered the handlers or whoever was in her way until she got what she wanted. Marching around that sprawling kennel, this one was clearly in command. A caterpillar-size being, whose tail looked like a pair of false eyelashes, she was a street fighter.

This was one tough little dog. She carried on like J.Lo if she didn't get enough attention. She rolled on the carpet, tugged at your skirt, scratched your leg, licked your fingers, trotted onto your lap, nudged you with her whole head. She danced up and down the hallways like a "look at me, look at me" spoiled brat.

Jazzy was scheduled with Paula's vet for his annual teeth cleaning, so he was doing an overnighter. I kissed him good-bye. I then lifted this other little furball with one hand to kiss her, too.

Paula warned me, "She's so small. Be careful you don't drop her."

The worry wasn't would I drop her, the worry was would she drop *me*! She wriggled and pawed at my palm ceaselessly. She wanted out. I couldn't stop staring at her. I was fascinated.

"She's delicious," I said.

I named her Juicy.

And I put her in my handbag.

My visit had been overlong, and I was late. I was due at a cocktail party back in New York. It was for Representative Katherine Harris, that Florida lady who, in earlier days, was in charge of those famous hanging, dimpled, now-you-see-'em-now-you-don't chads that nearly gored Bush. Up from Florida, Congressperson Harris was working our town.

The Metropolitan Club is austere, elegant, and wall-to-wall old hat. It's from the turn of the century. A ritzy private club where the average age of those who belong is deceased. Dogs are absolutely not members.

Juicy was so little that she could fit in a pocket, and that's about where I hid her. Inside my jacket. The jacket was short-sleeved because it was a warm night. I actually stuck Juicy under my armpit.

Katherine Harris was full of life. She shook my hand vigorously and raced about, smartly greeting everyone. I asked her where she gets her strength and how she jumps around on these superskinny high heels. She said, "I always wear spikes, but I love campaigning and I love meeting strangers, even though it means standing two hours on shoes like these."

Unfortunately, she'd shaken my hand a bit too vigor-

ously. I ran inside the ladies' room to see if Juicy was okay.
Not suffocating. She was fine. It was back to the ballroom.

Katherine relived with me how Florida's famous Primary
Day screwed up its voting procedures: "People didn't realize
my secretary of state job was an elected one. I didn't report
to Jeb Bush. I'd been elected statewide. I had total auton-
omy in overseeing the ballot.

"We allocated thirty-two million to fund the equipment,
and sixty-five other counties got it right. It wasn't the equipment, it was the people. They just couldn't plug into the
system."

Juicy had shifted position. I had to get out of there fast,
but I still needed to get a usable quote from this lady for the
column. To ensure Juicy not falling out, I was holding my
arm in an awkward position, as though it had been broken
then poorly reset, while we talked about Katherine Harris's
makeup.

She looked perfect. The makeup, a source of jokes when
she'd been on TV every night, was soft. So why those karate
chops about her lipstick and eyeliner?

"I don't know," she said with a smile. "I never changed
my makeup. Not one bit. What I was wearing then is exactly what I have on right now. It must be something in
television lighting or the computer technology that I don't
understand. Possibly I need some expert in that area to advise me.

"The point is, I don't fuss about myself at all. If I'm up at
eight-fifteen, I'm at the office eight-thirty. And I put the

makeup on in the car. At a traffic light. Those men who were criticizing me were wearing more makeup than I was."

With Juicy flouncing around under my armhole and slipping rapidly, I bounded for the exit. As I made haste, her fluffy raggy feathery tail fell out of my sleeve. I doubled it up and shoved it back, but it kept flopping out of my short sleeve and down my arm. A blue-haired senior who saw me rushing for the stairs commented: "Dear, you must try shaving."

Juicy made your heart stop. The body, such as it was, all eleven and a half inches of it, was all-over black. Her head, which if you cupped it in your hands, with the ears, beard, mustache whiskers, and sideburns smoothed away, was the size of, maybe, a walnut. The head was silver-blue. The fluffy rear end and tips of the teeny paws, coppery beige. Bunched on the floor, this was a living breathing feather. If you pulled it flat and stretched it full to its maximum, it wasn't even the length of feather an opera singer would stick in her chignon.

I couldn't understand how the Great Creator could have made anything so delicious. With Juicy I lost all sense of reason. Sanity became just a word in *Webster's*. I wanted to put this thing into a pie plate. I wanted to eat her with a spoon.

My one hand, extending thumb to middle finger, about closed around her neck. When she rumpled herself into a snaillike ball, it looked like an earmuff. Not sufficient fur for a neck piece. Just enough for an earmuff.

On the street, strangers suddenly stopped to make my acquaintance. To introduce me to their hulking Newfoundland, who was eyeing my gorgeous Juicy as an hors d'oeuvre. To make goo-goo eyes at my baby. To ask the same questions: Is she a boy or girl? How old is she? How big is she? What's her name? What *is* she? What is she? Hey, take a look, lady. For sure she's not a zebra.

The whole world loved Juicy. The whole world but Jazzy.

A day later, when he returned home, my house osmosed into the Bloods and the Crips. Two rival gangs. On one side a seven-pounder mama's boy, who voluntarily never strayed more than ten inches from my ankles. From age three months on he'd roamed the earth—or whatever there was of it in my apartment—as though he owned it. Which he did.

On the other side, in the tiny pink hair bow and sterling silver necklace with the teeny bone-shaped ID hanging off it—the Interloper. Forty ounces of pure selfish. A downright catty puppy. The size of a bird, the gut of a lion.

Like anyone who'd suddenly had a roommate unwillingly thrust upon him, Jazzy found his things newly scattered. His corner was usurped. His bones were not where he'd left them. He was battling for turf.

We set down his 'n' hers food bowls. Juicy only wanted his. We bought matching beds. Juicy only wanted to curl up in his. We had two identical carry bags. The one Jazzy favored was always the one Juicy dove into. Put out two chew sticks, Juicy would run away with his. Put down yet another chew stick, smack under Jazzy's nose, Juicy would race from wherever she was and tear that, too, away from him.

The household was very careful about not overloving Juicy Adams in the presence of Jazzy Adams. I'd studied how you must always cuddle the older one first so he doesn't feel upstaged by the younger arrival. Even if the sole purpose was to see Juicy, whoever came to my home was told: "Say hello to Jazzy first. Fuss over Jazzy first. Pick up Jazzy first. Rumple Jazzy first."

Forget it. Jazzy was into Attitude. The heretofore mama's boy was a spurned lover. The more I'd try to pet him or coax him or hold him, the more he basically told me: "Up yours." This dog couldn't have been more explicit if he'd stuck his paw to his nose and wiggled his pads at me.

Jazzy was retaliating. I took him to a bridal shower, and the biggest gift was from him. A colleague brought her Yorkie, whom Jazzy knows, by for a playdate, and Jazzy hustled smack up to my colleague's white shoe and left his mark. Hurrying out, this gal asked, "Was that an opinion of my work?"

Jazzy had been invited to a small dinner on a friend's terrace. The friend had a Jack Russell. The Jack Russell was instantly taken up by Juicy. Result? Jazzy developed a nervous tummy on a cushion and an indoor rug. Critiqued the host: "It seems not to be in its proper form. It's *Seeping*." I had to buy a new cushion and rug. That one dinner cost me four hundred dollars. The menu had been only pork and salad. Not worth four hundred dollars.

Jazzy would parade around the perimeter of whatever room I was in. He'd meander in circles. Not so wide that I could miss he was right there. He stayed underfoot. If I paid him no mind, he'd narrow the circles. Inch closer but always out of grabbing range. When minutes went by and I didn't make some effort to reach out, he'd wander smack up to me. Stand directly at my foot but not make a sound, not pay me any attention. In fact, deliberately stare off into some far-away yonder. The instant I'd reach out, he'd scamper away. Go after him, he'd scurry so deep under a table he couldn't be gotten to.

How could something with a brain so small be so skill-fully devious? Natural instinct or formulaic plan? I stared at this skein of hair. After he'd repeated this game and made a fool of me over and over, it finally got through that this was no isolated knee-jerk response. This Yorkshire terrier, who without me to feed him, bathe him, groom him, walk him, exercise him, house him would not survive, knew exactly what he was doing.

Teaching me a lesson was what he was doing. He was angry. Angry that I'd brought in his midget relative. Angry that there was another heart for me to hold. Angry that he now had to divide the attention.

Call him, he wouldn't come. Toss a sock with a ball

knotted in it for his preferred game of fetch, and he'd look at me like "Fetch you!"

Jazzy, no longer the Lion King, had become a pussycat. Instead of dominating, he cowered. Instead of barking at the new boarder, he whimpered. Instead of taking command, he ran for help.

Juicy's tiny mouth would lock onto his toy and her toy. If a third was tossed, she'd bounce onto that, too. To try and get her to leave his favorite basket of favorite playthings alone, I went shopping for squeaky rubber hamburgers, plush animals, and fake furry fetch whatevers appropriate for Juicy's size and interest. Items which might last more than six minutes and which she couldn't mangle into fragments. I was on a pilgrimage. Find a toy to engage her mind and body—and, incidentally, save my sanity. I had to give this dominatrix a doggy SAT. Test her. Did she prefer to chew? Did she prefer to squeak something? Did she prefer to run? Seemed she preferred all three, providing they were what Jazzy preferred. I remember reporting on Rudy Giuliani's divorce from second wife, Donna Hanover. Her court papers said Donna needed twelve hundred dollars a month for the upkeep of Goalie, their golden. I now knew why. Santa's playroom didn't have the junk I had.

If two of Jazzy's precious slobbery things looked like they were about to grab his attention, Juicy would race maniacally to nail them before he did. She'd put an end of each in her mouth just so he couldn't get them. She'd then run behind a chair and hide them. If he went for them, she'd pick both up again in her teeny jaws, and if I threw a third, she'd open that mouth, lose the other two, and clamp onto the third just so he couldn't have it.

I explained to her the parable of the monkey who had a banana and saw a second one and grabbed that also. Then, high in the tree, he saw another clump of fruit. Tucking his existing bananas under each arm, the monkey reached high over his head for the third one. Result? He lost the first two.

Juicy, unimpressed with my parable, went ahead with nailing whatever she wanted. If Jazzy did manage to get to it ahead of her, she'd grab onto whatever end was hanging loose and never let go. Never never. She'd tug and tug and finally wrench it away or run side by side with him, almost caving in on top of him, while they both kept it in their mouths. Never would she let go.

If she glommed on to his squeaky toy first, she'd run and wedge it into some minute corner where he couldn't go. He'd walk to and fro in front of her, growling. I'd have to get flat on the floor, grab his squeaky toy away from her personally, and give it to him. He wouldn't do it himself. Mike Tyson he wasn't.

The situation, plain and simple, was that I couldn't handle such drama. If I gave to one of my babies, I would trip over myself trying to soothe and smooth the other because I felt so disloyal. Immediately after ruffling Juicy for a few minutes, I'd go to pick up Jazzy. The difference was, Juicy had a streetwalker's insides. She'd go to whoever paid the price. The price being feeding her, playing with her, giving her attention. But Jazzy the Manipulator let me know what he thought of my bumbling. Not content with giving me the finger, he'd offer up his whole body. Every time I reached out he'd walk away from me.

Juicy was creating havoc.

I had done this for Jazzy. I had imported Juicy for Jazzy, and Jazzy was hating it—and her. I loved Jazzy. I adored this dog. This dog was my life. I lived, breathed, and ate this dog. This dog was my child. I wanted him happy, and he wasn't happy. I couldn't stand it.

Two weeks to the day, I returned Juicy to the breeder.

It fell to Reggie to drive Juicy back to Connecticut. The morning we were packing up her little belongings was a bad morning. Reggie is a tall strapping guy. Even his eyes were moist. When I kissed Juicy's tiny exquisite face and nestled her right into Reggie's big outstretched palm, I could barely bear it. Not to hear her scratching at my closed closet door ever again? No more to feel those hair-thin filaments which are her foot bones as she scampered across me? The house was like there'd been a death in the family. Nazalene and I were clutching one another. I was crying.

"I've tried so hard, and I can't make it work," I said to Paula on the phone. "I've tried to give half of myself all to Jazzy and give equally the other half of myself all to Juicy, and I can't make it work. They don't get along and I'm torn apart. I'm a disaster area."

I, who basically did not need a second animal around and who had no wish to be living in a dog run, was a mess. The groomer was saying this was twice as much work. The housekeeper was admitting it was definitely more work. The building employees, who'd had the pleasure when Juicy's manners were bad, were suggesting I probably hadn't thought how much more work this would be. Jazzy, for whom I'd undertaken this whole project and whom I loved more than life, was unhappy. My once self-centered only hound was now glum. Sullen. No longer playful. Upset. Not loving me.

Previously Jazzy never left my side. If I was in the tub, he was in the john. If I sat at my desk, he curled into a snail in his bed right next to it. If I zipped through the house, he trotted at my ankle. When I was away, I'd ease his separation anxiety by calling home. When he heard my voice, he barked and licked the phone.

I'd flitted around the country promoting my book, *The Gift of Jazzy*, and Jazzy had gone everywhere with me. Since the book was about him, the programs grudgingly accepted me as the person who showed up with their Guest, but what they wanted was *him*. He got the close-ups. On a Fox TV news interview, all you saw were my hands holding him. The rest of the time it was a tight shot on his face. No idea why I'd bothered with hair and makeup.

Every two days it had been a different city, different hotel, different room layout. I don't even remember what city it was that I had an L-shaped suite. I only remember that in the middle of the night I awoke realizing I hadn't left a water bowl anywhere for my roommate. I stumbled out of bed, located water in the minibar, poured it into a decorative pot that was on the coffee table, and opened the door to the john preparatory to placing it on the floor. Wrong door. It let me right out into the hotel's eighteenth-floor hallway and slammed behind me. Maybe other travelers trot around inside their locked hotel rooms at night with keys in their nighties, but I don't. There I was, a true vision, standing in the corridor facing an elevator in unpressed see-through sleepwear that was wet. The water had sloshed on me when the door closed. I ended up having to summon a bellboy and . . . Don't ask. . . .

Everyone did segments about Jazzy. He showed up for book signings. He faced a battery of news cameras when he walked the red carpet for a Harry Potter movie opening. He posed for layouts. He sat on a special pillow at the front table at Le Cirque, dining off porcelain and crystal with his menu of chicken breast and Evian, as *The New York Times* snapped his picture for a Sunday feature. A reporter and photographer flew from *The Washington Post* for two days just to follow Jazzy. His actual opinions were sought in magazines.

Jazzy had truly become a VID. Very Important Dog. When New York's Board of Tourism did a Paint the Town Red promotion, they asked me to dress Jazzy in red and pose with him. A New Yorkie, get it? When Wynton Marsalis,

Willie Nelson, Ray Charles, Eric Clapton, B. B. King, Laurence Fishburne headed a Jazz at Lincoln Center Festival, I was asked to bring Jazzy as the mascot. When furrier Dennis Basso gave a fashion show for eight-hundred people—Diana Ross, Liza Minnelli, those Hilton girls—he asked for Jazzy to come wearing his golden sable. "I insist he attend. He's my client!" he said. *Us Weekly* does a fashion police segment where VIPs rate other VIPs' clothes. Jazzy was booked one week as the celebrity critic to give his opinion of shoes. Growls like "That one's a dog . . . The back of my paw to that one . . ." The late Ismail Merchant of the Oscar-winning producing team Merchant-Ivory had borrowed him for a documentary. It was the Park Avenue pooch in his couture in a chauffeured block-long superstretch limo.

Now, from being the canine Russell Crowe, with unending groomers and handlers and dressers and fluffers and personal photographers seven days a week, it went to lying in his doggy bed in the kitchen sulking. He'd honor me by accepting treats, but that was about it for the high life.

For years we'd gone almost nowhere without the other. Now, he made it plain he didn't think enough attention was being paid to him. His eyes drooped. His tail was down. I had a depressed Yorkie.

However, the situation that had created the problem— his being an only dog—had still not been resolved. Nothing had changed. He still needed a companion. I still had been correct in my basic assessment. So . . . what to do? Start all over again? Try to break in yet another species? Search around to find a different brand, a new unfamiliar pet with maybe a more docile personality?

Juicy was lying there in my gut. Had I gone to a heart specialist, Juicy would have shown up on my EKG.

I understand this is not precisely the same attraction Jessica Simpson has for Nick Lachey, but what could I do. Whacked-out or not whacked-out, I was in love.

Jazzy, however, was not.

A week later I called Paula again. Paula knew. She'd been waiting for this call. She knew this little baby had been born for me. She'd promised herself never to give away this caterpillar, to keep her forever for me because she knew that, somehow, down the road, I had to have Juicy.

Back came Juicy, and we took her to the vet for a once-over. He pronounced her a healthy animal. He also told us, "She's gained half an ounce." Other than that half an ounce, nothing about this 2.5.5-pound descendant of wolves had changed. My ten-month-old was running rings around the three-and-three-quarters-year-old, mature, elder statesdog Jazzy. She was like a laser. This angel face didn't obsess over anything, her doggy brain didn't weigh options, she never wasted efforts getting even, she was totally attitudeless. She didn't seem to hold it against me that she'd been shuttled back and forth from orphanage to foster home. She just reverted to character. She went straight for what she wanted and took it.

Jazzy already owned 5.5 rooms of my apartment, but the very day Juicy came back to us, you could see Jazzy again feel himself losing control. With the return of this adorable second dog's feistiness came the return of our beloved Only Dog's crankiness.

Someone said Jazzy was Joey, my late husband. Sort of laid-back. And, they said, Juicy was me. She wanted what she wanted. She was independent, she was single-minded, she cut through the B.S. That's not necessarily any compliment. It's just what they said.

Again I did everything the books say to do in order to keep your original older pet as the Top Dog. The only problem was, Juicy didn't have a library card. Juicy didn't read those same books. Juicy instantly ascended to alpha position.

If Jazzy was drinking water and Juicy decided she was thirsty? She simply wriggled her way in, nudged him aside, and lapped foreleg to foreleg with him. He was snoozing happily on a pillow near an open window and it came to her that this breezy spot was a lovely place to be? She just hopped, rabbit-style, right onto that pillow, and if her hop landed her smack on his stomach, so be it. Jazzy would growl and, without enough room for them both, slink away.

Juicy wanted what she wanted, but she also wanted to be friendly. She followed Jazzy everywhere. She wanted to share his space. To be with him. Cranky Jazzy returned the favor one morning by nipping her. She yipped in pain. I screamed. Jazzy hid. Juicy shook.

Animal behaviorists warned me it takes time. You can't simply foist a second dog onto a first dog. Pet psychologist Warren Eckstein told me, "Be patient. You must do it bit by bit. You should have introduced them on neutral turf." I'd done that. They'd first met with Paula the breeder.

Ivan Kovacs the trainer told me, "You have to let them work it out." I *was* letting them work it out. The problem was, they weren't working it out.

A dog handler said to me, "You have to understand it takes awhile." Well, I understood that, and I had taken this while.

A professional animal behaviorist told me, "Get the opposite sex, get a younger, smaller creature, so Jazzy feels superior." Well, I'd done all that.

I knew there was an understanding between animals. I also knew I needed my animals. At least I needed the one I had. Jazzy made me smile. He cuddled in my arms or plopped into my lap and relieved whatever stress I had. He lightened my heart. Often a day starts before I have a chance to start. Many a morning I've felt everything was out of control. An argument, another misunderstanding—and Jazzy would curl up against me or on top of me. I'd rub his stomach, massage his neck, kiss his ears, and think once again, Oh, how could God have made anything so huggable?

However, my home was in turmoil. I loved loved loved little Juicy. Nazalene kept stroking her tiny face with "Ohhh, she's so sweet. Give her another chance. Try another few days." Then Jazzy would nip her again. Then Jazzy would go off alone again. Then Reggie would say: "Jazzy is not himself anymore. That beautiful dog we love is different. His whole personality has changed. Jazzy's going to get sick from unhappiness. You're going to kill Jazzy if you don't send Juicy back."

I sent Juicy back.

Then something happened to Jazzy. Suddenly he wouldn't play. He wouldn't respond if you tossed a ball. He didn't run when he saw us. He wouldn't cuddle. Now he was eating even less. He wasn't enjoying anything. He was listless. There could have been only one reason. Only one element had changed in his life. Juicy was gone. Juicy was gone for seven days. Jazzy was downcast for seven days.

I brought Juicy home again. She thanked me by peeing on my foot. In preparation for her arrival, Nazalene had washed the kitchen floor. Juicy ran right through the suds and the slosh, and her little paw prints went all over the house. I thought, Is this to be my lot for eternity? To walk in wet for the rest of my life?

I finished my walk into the kitchen, and there I saw sweet Miss Juicy performing a Monica Lewinsky on happy Mr. Jazzy. And I realized: Juicy, sweetie, baby, looks like you're with us forever.

But forgetting those two, there was even a transformation in me. The lesson I'd learned from Jazzy, the newly happy camper, was: Life is a cabaret.

THREE

You Never Lose the Ones You Love

A few weeks later Jazzy was dead.

Dead.

He was dead.

My Jazzy was dead.

Jazzy hadn't been ill. He hadn't been feeling poorly. He'd not been placed in any dangerous or stressful situation. He'd not been born with some dormant potentially deadly condition that could come into play at any moment. My precious protected beautiful Jazzy had not come face-to-face with debilitating fear. There was no accident. He did not ingest poison, eat something indigestible, or suffer heatstroke. He did not find himself up against some predatory beast. He did not get stung or bitten. He had not run away. He did not fall into evil hands. He was not beaten.

And he was dead.

His age was three years and eleven months.

He hadn't even been allowed to grow old and frail.

And he was dead.

It was August 17. September 29 would have been his fourth birthday.

My pain was such that I lay in bed in a fetal position.

It had been a stifling summer weekend. Like any city-bound mother who desperately loves her children, I wanted the best for my babies. That, even though it meant my sacrificing their companionship, signified cool air, greenery, outdoors, romps in open fields in the company of those they knew well. Doggy friends and human friends.

I was obliged to be in the city working—actually on this very book, which the publishers had decided should be the continuation of my life with my precious Jazzy—and so I sent my little family to doggy camp in the country.

These were professionals. They were familiar. When I'd sent Jazzy every Thursday for socializing, this had been the group in charge. When I gave him his first birthday party in my home with celebrities and their dogs, they ran it. When I opened my first boutique, Jazzy's, in his name, in Macy's, they were on duty. Bette Midler's Jack Russell had gone to them, Liam Neeson's Molly had gone to them, Ingrid Rossellini's dachshund, Yuma, had gone to them. At one point Blaine Trump's Yorkie, Pearl, and Joan Rivers's bunch had been regulars. Never never ever would I have entrusted Jazzy to strangers or even some close friend. He and his sister, Juicy, were personally watched over and transported hand to hand, from my outstretched arms into the trustworthy arms of those who had been involved in Jazzy's care since December 9, 1999, the day he came to me.

Nazalene loved Jazzy as much as I. Exactly seven days after my husband of forty years left me, a friend delivered this three-month-old cowering puppy to help me through my loss. From the magical moment that trembling thimble wriggled into our bones, Nazalene had been there to feed him, hug him, warm him, stuff him under her shirt, tend him, comfort him. My housekeeper was his personal nanny. If I had to go away, she took him to her home, and I, Jazzy's mama, always double-checking when this baby was out of my sight, would call daily from everywhere in the world. I'd phone from China, Africa, ship-to-shore on board the *Queen Mary 2*'s transatlantic crossing just to hear him bark.

This particular Saturday and Sunday, Nazalene needed to be away from home herself. She had committed to an out-of-town family wedding. And me, I was stuck with a round-the-clock work schedule. So, I took a deep breath. I thought, Okay, it's only one long weekend. It's fresh air. Good health. We're not talking strangers. We're talking handlers who know Jazzy and Juicy and who Jazzy and Juicy know.

Jazzy never came back to me.

What came back to me was his cold blood-caked body.

He was handed over dead.

My Jazzy was dead.

He and Juicy had left on their usual socializing day,

Thursday. Thursday's routine didn't vary. Those mornings Jazzy and Juicy were hand-carried downstairs to Reggie. Never were they farmed off to one of the building employees or asked to be watched over by a friendly neighbor who was coincidentally going down in the elevator at the same time. Either Nazalene or I would hold them in our arms and hand them directly into Reggie's. Reggie, whom they've also known since Day One, would set them next to him in the front seat. My car. A car they knew well. A Reggie they knew well. A routine they knew well. Reggie would personally deliver them to the day-care handlers, whose city facility was barely ten minutes away. That script was followed religiously, so they felt safe and protected and happy. They were used to these Thursdays. They knew the friends they would see. They knew all the players and all the smells. They knew where they were going. They knew what to expect. They knew they were coming back.

This one Thursday my babies were not going to the usual city facility but, instead, were embarking on a two-and-a-half-hour trip to the handlers' upstate country farm. As a result it was agreed they'd transport Jazzy and Juicy with their own people in their own van. People familiar with the drill, who knew the way and made the trip often. Thus, their own employees collected Jazzy and Juicy. No Reggie. No car that they knew.

I'd gone out on an early appointment. When I returned in the afternoon, Nazalene was upset. She said, "Jazzy didn't want to go. He fought like a tiger. Even the doorman saw that. Juicy was okay, Jazzy wasn't."

We knew Jazzy never wanted to go anywhere away from me or without me. He accepted Thursdays easily only because he knew the routine.

"Do you think he might've been upset this morning because it wasn't Reggie?" asked Nazalene. "It was some strange driver."

"I don't know," I said. "I never thought about that."

"And it was some strange vehicle. Sort of like a little truck."

We stood still and stared at one another. We suddenly realized the sounds would have been different, the look would have been different, the smells different. The driver was different. "Y'know what?" I said very quietly. "What just occurred to me? This doggy pickup van probably had cages."

"Cages?" repeated Nazalene.

"Cages. This is a professional doggy transport. Equipped to carry more than one or two dogs at a time. Even big dogs. He was probably put in a cage."

"Jazzy's never been in a cage."

"I know." We both fell silent a moment, then: "So, Jazzy didn't know where he was going, didn't know with whom he was going, and certainly wasn't accustomed to a cage."

"So he must have been stressed out."

"He must have been terrified."

Nazalene kept obsessing she was to blame. If not for this

wedding, our two babies wouldn't have had to go away. We both fretted about it. We were torturing ourselves. We finally came to thinking that, since we were both troubled, we'd send Reggie to bring the dogs back. I said, "Look, somehow, between us, we'll find some way of watching over them until Monday. Call the farm and tell them Reggie is coming to collect them."

That was Thursday, August 14, 2003. The day electricity over a huge chunk of North America went out. Fifty million of us were affected, up as far as Canada and from the Northeast all the way to Ohio. Like everyone in New York City, I had no lights, no phones, no running water, no TV, no AC. My lights dimmed then surged then went out totally. Regular phones dead. Cell phones dead. Car phones dead. Streetlights, highway lights, dead. Trains, dead. E-mails, dead. Faxes, dead. No communications whatsoever. No way to check on my babies. No way to check on anybody or anything.

Twenty-six hours later, Friday at 6:00 P.M., service in my area was sufficiently restored to allow intermittent telephone connections.

The first time I could get through I called the farm. Everyone okay? My angelic charges survive the ordeal all right? Is it harmonious up there? Yes, I was told, all is well.

I did not really like the way the call went. It was quick. Too quick. The other end didn't enlarge our exchange by so much as a breath. It went exactly like this—I can still hear it in my head:

Me, excitedly: "Hi. You all okay up there?"

Them, quietly: "We're good."

Me, babbling: "Wow, wasn't this something? I had candles luckily, but it was some mess. Is there anything I can do for you, anything you need? My babies okay?"

Them, carefully: "We're good."

A millisecond of silence, then, from me: "I hope Jazzy and Juicy don't miss me too much. I was worrying they were maybe a little stressed out about the trip up there. . . . They doing all right?"

"Everything's fine."

Fine?!

A significant portion of our civilization had just gone over twenty-four hours with no water, refrigeration, electricity, lights, air, fans, TV, cells, streetlamps, stoplights, stoves, microwaves, washers, driers, irons, elevators, vacuums, transportation, trains, planes, buses. And that was the whole assessment of what this group had been through? Fine?! They were fine? The dogs were fine?

Fine?!

This power outage had been so all-consuming that it will be recorded in history books. When power was ultimately restored, half the United States took to jabbering to friends, family, strangers, anybody about where they were when It happened. They couldn't stop blabbing about what they'd gone through, how they'd handled It, what miseries they'd overcome. Everyone had a story. Everyone wanted to talk. Me, I'd sliced my lip when, in the darkness, scrabbling around for candles and flashlights, I'd somehow smacked into a wall. Half of America and Canada was spilling over to relate what they had endured. Everyone was checking in with everyone. We all reached out to the aged, the infirm, the babysitters, the petsitters, those who hadn't been able to get home, those who'd had no food, those who'd gotten stuck in elevators. The whole world was trading hairy experiences.

Jazzy's handlers alone remained eerily taciturn. It was as though they were unwilling to share what had gone on way up in the country with the dogs they were boarding. Impossible as this seemed, it was almost as though they'd not even been way up in the country with the dogs they were boarding. It was almost as though they had call forwarding and answered their telephone in some place far removed from what had happened. Their demeanor and flat, calm, unexcited voices were sharply out of sync with everybody else's. Their eagerness not to speak much in hopes I'd get off the line—what they were *not* saying—pushed some damage control buzzer in my head. But I didn't know what. I had to dismiss it, mostly because I didn't know what to do about it.

No uplifting carefree lightness washed over me when I hung up. "Fine" met my nagging worry but afforded no sense of satisfaction. In my head I tried to lay the abruptness on the fact that they'd had their own problems dealing with the power failure and had probably been besieged with owners calling. I tried. It didn't work, but I tried.

A minor current underlying my passive acceptance of

their odd behavior was that I had history with these people. They'd previously been annoyed by my repeat check-ins. They never dared be overtly rude to me, but they had once said: "We haven't time to be on the phone. Our job is to be out taking care of the dogs." Another shot they'd given me was cloaked in the half joke "God, you're so hyper when it comes to Jazzy. If he got a cold you'd probably call an ambulance."

These two exchanges had made me sensitive to their position. When last they'd expressed it, I had entertained the thought that maybe they were right. Since others had also chided me on being overprotective, I restrained myself from phoning the farm again Saturday.

Sunday he was dead.

This healthy strong mama's boy, whose face was on my computer, whose photos covered my walls, who curled his paws around my neck in bed, who never voluntarily left my side, who I loved more than anything in my life, who was my only family, the main creature left in this world I could call my own, who hadn't yet reached his fourth birthday, was dead!

I couldn't talk about it. I couldn't bear it. I could not believe it. Even now I would never believe it had I not seen with my own eyes his lifeless being, covered in the blood that had poured from that tiny body.

Approximately ten weeks earlier he'd been thoroughly checked. And his vet told me: "You've got a really great dog there. A tough strong fellow. He's wonderfully healthy."

And now he was dead.

A terrible scene played and replayed in my mind. It caromed through my brain. I had not been able to shake this since the day it happened, maybe two months earlier. It had been a springtime Sunday afternoon. I'd been walking both babies. Out of the corner of my eye I could see a lady. She stopped and watched as I cuddled Jazzy while reciting his name in a specifically playful never-ending always-changing singsong, "Jazzy Jazzy Jazzzzzy, Jazeeeee, Jazzybaby, Jazzypoo, Jazz Jazz Jazz Jazzy." It was our fun game, and his tail wagged double time when he heard it. She came closer. She said to me: "I know who you are. And I know who your dog is. You really love him very much, right?"

I answered half flippantly: "I'd kill myself if anything happened to him."

This lady then said quietly: "Don't ever love anything that much. If you do, God will take it away from you."

It was *wow*! Like getting stabbed in the chest. This two-second street-side exchange I could not forget. The VCR in my brain jammed in that spot. No matter how I pushed, the Eject button just would not work.

I'd read somewhere that we are all in different states of consciousness and that we all have different dreams. The end product of that being, whatever nightmare this lady was specifically rewinding was not necessarily one that included me. She was obviously stuck in some tragedy of her own and, unconsciously, projecting it onto me. Still, I couldn't shake it off.

From then on I stayed cloaked in some inexplicable garment of heaviness. I tried to ward off this black weight by erecting a divine wall. I immersed myself in gratitude, as though some jingo could antidote this dark cloud. Over and over I thanked God for His goodness and His blessings to my household and especially for His bringing and then caring for these two loving innocent creatures who had brought so much to me. I silently explained what Jazzy stood for in my life. How he'd filled the void after my husband and my mother left me. How I had nobody else. No siblings, children, cousins, uncles, nobody. How I was alone. How all I had was Jazzy and Juicy.

I told Him I knew Jazzy and Juicy were God-sent, and that if they came to me under His direction then it stood to reason they were under His protection and I knew He therefore maintained and sustained them because He was All.

But just to make sure, when those small warm bodies would burrow into me at night, I'd lift up a corner of the blanket to check if Jazzy was breathing.

Sunday morning, around 11:00 A.M. of the very day Jazzy was taken from me forever, I was in the thick of battling this unseen unfathomable burden. I am not superstitious. I am not a believer in the esoteric spells of black magic. But the karma was bad. I'd gone out for a short walk to clear my head since I was trying to write this book and nothing was coming through. I was blocked. The blockage had turned to fear. The fear had turned to terror. The terror had turned to: "That lady. What if she was right? What if because I love him so much he'll be taken away from me? What would I do? How do I handle it? How could I survive?"

This was some sort of sick hypnotic evil nameless voodoo. Still, there it was and I was under it.

I came home, and the phone rang. The strained voice of this caregiver I'd spoken with two days earlier. It was a scratchy cell phone with traffic sounds in the background. She said: "Jazzy's very sick. He's very sick. Cindy, Jazzy's very very sick."

Very sick? Very very sick? My child? What the hell was she talking about? Jazzy was "very very sick"? She'd used two *very*s. "Very very sick." How did he suddenly get "very very sick"? When had he become even a little bit sick? Saturday? Friday, when she'd used words so sparingly and told me he was "fine"?

"What are you talking about?" I asked. "What happened?"

"We don't know. He's expelling projectile blood. We've never seen something like this. We don't know what happened. Blood is pouring out of him everywhere."

"Jazzy?" I repeated stupidly. "My Jazzy?"

"Listen, he's very very sick," she repeated. "Pray."

"*Pray?* My dog is *that* sick?! *Very very* sick? Two months before he was superhealthy. Three days before he was great. I sent off a gorgeous healthy dog. Two days ago you told me he was 'fine.' You're telling me now I have a dog so sick that my only option is prayer?"

"He's very sick."

"*Very* sick? When did he get *this* sick? It takes a while to become *so* sick, so *very* sick. When did he suddenly start getting this sick?"

"Look, we're on the highway right now."

That was the next link in the chain of statements that made no sense. "What do you mean 'highway'? Why isn't he in a hospital? Where's the vet on duty?"

"No vet here that can handle this."

Next statement that didn't make sense. No vet? Boarding dogs in a place with no vet?

"We're driving him into the Animal Medical Center," she said.

Next statement that again made no sense. I shouted: "The Animal Medical Center is in New York City. You're near Albany. Two and half hours away."

"We're giving him intravenous in the car. We'll meet you there."

"Intravenous? In the car?"

"He's dying, Cindy. Blood is pouring out of him on both ends. Projectile blood."

"He's gone from being very sick to dying? And you're *driving* my dying dog two and a half hours, all the way from upstate into a facility in the city? I don't understand."

"We're taking him to the best hospital."

"Why isn't he already in a hospital? Where is the hospital up there?"

"We're heading for the hospital."

I was crazed. I shouted: "Where's Juicy? Who has my Juicy?"

"We do."

I didn't understand, but there wasn't time for me to try to understand. It was raining. I threw on clothes, hired a car and driver, grabbed two cells in case one should go down, my in-case phone list, and ran out in fifteen minutes. Since I was driving in the opposite direction, coming from New York City, I said I'd meet them on the highway at whichever point we crossed each other.

A normal Sunday night in the summer is bumper to bumper. This one was even worse. It was the Sunday night following the two-day blackout. Travelers were checking on loved ones. And it was pouring. Traffic was barely moving.

I dialed every two minutes. I wasn't in the car twenty minutes when the voice of Jazzy's caregiver came through on a scratchy phone. She said: "He won't make it to the city. We're heading for a veterinarian hospital we know in Long Island."

"He won't make it? You have my dog who's dying, you're coming from upstate all the way into New York City, and you're now peeling off into Long Island!?"

"The vet there is the best. And we already have a catheter in him."

"A catheter?" And then again, "Juicy! Where actually is Juicy?"

"Here with us."

They gave me the approximate name and whereabouts of this hospital. I called my assistant, Marcee, at home and told her to find out the phone number, exact name, exact location, and directions to get there. My traffic lanes were solid parking lots. I then called their car to tell them I didn't know how long it would take me to get there.

They didn't answer.

I called again.

They didn't answer.

In my panic I was punching numbers too quickly. My phone jammed.

I tried the other cell phone.

They answered. "Jazzy's dead" was what they said.

I couldn't hear clearly with the traffic din and the patter of the rain. "What? Say again?"

"Jazzy's dead."

"Jazzy's *dead?*"

"Yes."

"You mean, my dog Jazzy . . . is dead?"

"He's dead."

"Jazzy is dead? Are you sure?"

"Yes."

Between Marcee working her home phones and me on my two cells, we located my own vet. His hospital is only six blocks from my home and is open 24/7. After my several almost hysterical calls, he said to bring Jazzy there.

My car got off at the next exit, turned round, and headed back. I arrived ten minutes ahead of the two who were carrying Jazzy. There had been neither time nor thought to call anyone to be with me. I stood out front . . .

in the street . . . in the rain. Waiting for him. Alone. Facing this tragedy by myself.

The caregivers' blue pickup truck pulled up alongside the entrance.

One of the two cradled my now lifeless lifeline in her arms. He was wrapped in big white blankets that were soaked through with his blood. I touched him. I stroked him. I hugged him. I kissed him.

The moment was awkward. It was nighttime. An empty waiting room in an animal hospital. Sterile. Antiseptic. Unwelcoming. Rendered doubly so because these were the quiet hours. The two caregivers stood there in the center. Rooted. Not moving. One holding this mountain of blankets that held my dead Jazzy. The other holding the overly quiet tiny body of Juicy. Two technicians emerged from somewhere inside to receive us. It. Him. Nobody said anything. What was there to say?

In the widening deafening silence, I eventually heard my own voice: "We lost Jazzy. Dr. Berman told me to bring him here and you'd know what to do."

The cool, professionally impersonal voice of a technician accustomed to dealing with death said, "Yes, we know. He told us."

The caregiver holding Jazzy appeared to be in shock. She was still standing still. In the center of the room. Holding him.

"Give them Jazzy," I said.

She gave them Jazzy.

The three of us—plus Juicy—went out into the rainy night.

There is an essay titled "The Rainbow Bridge." The anonymous author's words vary slightly depending on where you find it. It reads:

Just this side of Heaven is a place called the Rainbow Bridge. The Bridge connects Heaven and Earth. It is called the Rainbow Bridge because of its many colors. Just this side of the Rainbow Bridge is a land of meadows, hills, and valleys with lush green grass.

When a beloved animal dies who has been especially close to someone here, that pet goes to this place. There is always food and water and warm spring weather. All our special friends are warm and comfortable. The old and frail animals are young again. Those who are maimed are made whole and strong again. All the animals who had been ill are restored to health and vigor, just as we remember them in our dreams of days and times gone by.

The animals are happy and content, except for one small thing: They miss someone very special to them who had to be left behind. They are not with their special person who loved them on Earth.

They all run and play together, but the day comes when one suddenly stops and looks into the distance. The bright eyes are intent; the nose twitches; the eager body quivers. Suddenly he begins to break away from the group, flying over the green grass, his legs carrying him faster and faster. *You* have been spotted, and when you and your special friend finally meet, happy kisses rain upon your face, your hands again caress the beloved head. And you look once more into the trusting eyes of your pet, so long gone from your life but never absent from your heart.

Then you cross the Rainbow Bridge together . . .

Whoever wrote that had the soul of a poet.

But did it help?

No.

I loved this ball of fur more than anything I'd ever experienced. He absolutely was the love of my life.

I remembered his chin smack on the ground while the rest of him sloped *up*. He was like one of those Citroën cars. Tushy up high, and then suddenly that whole back end would collapse flat down, too.

I remembered that, when I'd felt in need of a TLC jolt, I'd reach out and that wet nose would smooch into my hand. Take a nap, he'd snuggle under my arm. Be lost in thought, he'd climb into my lap. The book *God's Messengers* postulates that if your pet is curled on your lap while you meditate, its brain waves also register "bliss, transcendence or enlightenment."

I remembered that he invariably rested with his head hanging down. And that he'd sleep with one paw on whichever of my parts was closest. I'd watch that tiny rib cage billow rhythmically. For some it's coke, others heroin. My drug of choice was this sweet living confection. He calmed me. He was my Prozac.

I loved him. I loved him. I loved him.

I'd squeeze both my arms around him. He'd wag his tail. He'd lick my face. Despite whatever troubles, he'd make me smile. You cannot know that emotion until you've fallen for one of these creatures who follows you with his eyes, who lights up at the sight of you, who trusts you implicitly, who asks only that you pet him.

For too long I'd known only the elderly and helpless. My husband, who for years was fragile, was now gone. My mother, who for years no longer recognized me, was now gone. My family, the face I ran home to, the one living breathing entity I knew loved me was my dog.

I remembered the day of a blizzard. We were entwined, hugging one another, facing a huge picture window. Jazzy didn't connect with the concept of glass. He tried to catch the snow with his paw. Nothing opens your heart as wide as the sight of a puppy playing.

I remembered how close to Juicy he'd recently grown. Like when she didn't appreciate getting her toenails clipped, he ran to her rescue and tugged at the groomer. Like when she became entangled in a bag's strap, he howled and scratched at the outside until we came running to release her.

After I lost Joey, coming into an empty house was spooky. I remembered how Jazzy filled that stillness. He also filled my thoughts. With my husband's relay of twenty-four-hour nurses, I'd never had to let myself in, so I never had keys. In my new life, because I had to run home and feed Jazzy, I developed the habit of double-checking to be sure I could get in my front door.

I remembered, I remembered . . . What didn't I remember? When my days were stressful, it was Jazzy who brought me healing. Jazzy who delivered the dose of comfort no medic could provide. I'd tumble him. Rub his fur against the grain. I'd lift him high over my head, set his paws down on my forehead, and we'd stare unblinkingly into one another's eyes.

When I was a kid, Rufus, my black Scottie, was killed by a car. The pain for me was intense. It took years for the healing to come. By the time I sensed I could deal with another dog, my husband was too frail. And so at this stage of my experience, this was my abiding love. It was the Abraham, Isaac, and Jacob syndrome. Joseph, the son of Jacob's old age, was the child he loved most.

I'd survived my husband's loss. I'd survived my mom's. Surviving Jazzy's stretched me to the breaking point.

My friend Judge Judy, who has an apartment only a few blocks from mine and whose shih tzu, Lulu, had playdates with Jazzy, came over. I said, "It's bizarre. After I lost Joey, friends worried that I was alone and so I got Jazzy. Then I worried that Jazzy was alone so I got Juicy. Now I lost Jazzy and I'm worried that Juicy's alone. I can't seem to get it right."

I showed her an overflowing cartonful of letters, sympathy cards, and homemade doggy Polaroids that had been sent me from all over the country.

"The fans have been wonderful. They've written thousands of letters. And I'm grateful for them. But can you believe someone wrote to say that I shouldn't wait? That I should get another Jazzy immediately. Can you imagine anything like that? How could anyone even suggest the thought of my taking in another dog to replace him?"

"You can't replace him," said practical, matter-of-fact Judy, who constantly makes decisions that affect people's lives. "You're not going to replace him. You're not even *trying* to replace him. Who said you're replacing him?"

"I feel sick at the thought of trying to love yet another dog."

"Look," she said in her trademark clipped way. "I had an elderly neighbor who lived alone. I always met him when he was out walking his black Scottie, Trevor. He adored Trevor. One morning I saw that this gentleman was totally changed. His brisk gait had slowed. His head was bowed. He shuffled. Eyes were downcast. He said he was forlorn.

"The dog had died. He said, 'I don't have Trevor anymore. My beloved Trevor is out of my life.'

"He had nobody to need him. He needed to be needed.

"So I said, 'So why don't you get another Trevor?'

"He said, 'How could I do that? I would feel disloyal. I mean, how can you replace your child?'

"I told him, 'Let's say you died. Wouldn't you want Trevor to have a good home? Somebody to love him?'

"He said, 'Yes. Of course.'

"So I said, 'I'm sure that's what he would want for you. Therefore, you now have to think of the reverse. Make believe you died and go get yourself another black Scottie.'

"He did. And you know what? He's happy again. The last time I saw him he said, 'I love him as much as I loved Trevor.'"

Mrs. Jerry Sheindlin, the TV personality now known internationally as Judge Judy, is a treasure. I am devoted to her. She has a message to give, she gives it. She has something to say, she says it. I knew what she was trying to do, and I was grateful.

Joan Rivers, my friend longer than either of us will admit we've been alive, also came over. When Joan lost her adored Yorkie, Spike, after nineteen years she told me: "Please . . . I can't even talk about it." She now owns three dogs, not one. Different breeds. She said, "It's my attempt to cushion any future pain."

I understood what they were doing. As I stood on the threshold of heartbreak, I kept remembering that opening myself to this dog had opened the door for love to walk in.

Parenting this seven-pound hairball that had warmed my bones and shared my home, I had witnessed pure truth. Jazzy embodied an openness that was no part of my own world of artifice and make-believe. In him I saw the naked emotion that I'd always taken care to mask. If he was lonely, the pain in his eyes was visible. If he felt needy, he didn't hide the hunger for attention. He was embarrassingly happy to see me when I came in. He wasn't ashamed to show fear. Not being a Yorkie, I hadn't instinctively known how to let down and demonstrate raw open loneliness or weakness. Me, I'd been conditioned. I knew to dissemble. The world in which I traveled went by one mantra: Never let the bastards see you sweat.

It was Jazzy who unlocked the way for me. What I could hold on to throughout that enemy season was the lesson my cherished Jazzy had left me. He'd placed his paw prints on my heart. He'd opened me to a new kind of love.

FOUR

Life Is Still Worth Living

 My husband, my mother, now my dog. Joey, Jessie, Jazzy. Jesus! I asked God what He's got against me.

So what happened?

I don't know.

I'll never know.

My vet suggested an autopsy. I said no. The mental picture of this little boy dissected on a cold slab, did me in. I took to my bed, sucking my thumb.

Twenty-four hours later my spirit could not rest. I had to try to know.

The autopsy basically ruled out what had *not* happened. No foul play. No shaken dog syndrome. No embolism, aneurysm, no any other ism. No heart failure.

So?

So why have I now only ashes in a sealed ivory urn on my bedroom bureau in place of warm furry pleasure with paws around my neck that made me feel less lost and lonely?

What they said—*all* they said—as we three stood awkwardly in the center of the animal hospital waiting room was "We don't know what happened. We've never seen anything like this before."

To devastated Paula, who'd brought Jazzy into the world, they said: "We've been in the business sixteen years. We never lost a dog before."

To them Paula said quietly: "Then you're lucky. I've been in this business forty years."

The autopsy reported *E. coli* in Jazzy's system. Me, I'd lay on the floor hand-feeding him a personally diced up spoon of cantaloupe, a crumb of a bagel with cottage cheese on it, so how did he get such a killer bacteria? Buckingham Palace didn't watch the Queen of England the way we monitored Jazzy. This was no barnyard cur who groveled for unclean scraps. Poached chicken breast in consommé with white rice. Not for me. For him. We looked hourly at his eyes, his mouth, his teeth, his nose. We checked his tushy. We sniffed his ears because a foul odor is supposedly symptomatic of something. We don't know what. We only know we kept sniffing In Case. We dressed him in monogrammed cashmere. We wiped his paws when he came in from the outside. We inspected his nails, his fur. We daily ran our fingers over every millimeter of his skin looking for whatever. He was constantly combed, brushed, groomed. I should be so cared for.

Where could he have gotten that?

They couldn't say. They didn't know.

Tests said its "probable" cause was HGG. A hypogastro-enteritis virus that can sweep through a little dog's organs and take them out fast—if his immune system is down.

And why would his immune system have been down?

The only answer the doctors could dredge up was "A partial factor is stress."

Whereas Juicy could eat live worms and be a contestant on *Fear Factor*, Jazzy was finicky. Thus, in an unfamiliar setting, Jazzy maybe didn't have food for two days.

Assuming he was hungry and by then gassed up, who knows if he got into some dead wild animal somewhere in the bushes? Who'd have seen or known? There're big dogs, small dogs. Hard to monitor one hundred acres. When it comes to little squiggly ones, it takes a village. Besides, a nanny doesn't watch the way a mother does.

The educated guess is, whatever unfolded inside him could have been reversed had the danger been assessed earlier. His symptoms weren't handled quickly enough. His caregivers first noticed signs at five that Sunday morning, almost twelve hours before I was informed. They took his temperature. It was low. He was cold. They wrapped him in blankets. They went for a heating pad. By eleven o'clock the situation had deteriorated. They started an IV drip so he didn't dehydrate. It all takes time. They did not speed him to a vet. They home-treated.

Whoopsing followed by bloody diarrhea is a signal something is going on internally. With such a confluence of symptoms, warning bells ring and dogs get raced to Emergency. When blood began pouring out of him, he should already have been in Emergency. Where were the professionals and equipment that would have saved him? The caregivers had said something to me on the cell phone like "The sophisticated facilities we need aren't here." Then why were they *there*?

They put Jazzy, his catheter, and Juicy into their pickup and headed toward the city. The traffic for that normally two-and-a-half-hour drive was impassable. And, were that possible, the rain had slowed it even more. The highway was a parking lot.

My Jazzy didn't make it.

In the tears, emptiness, and heartache that followed, one lone element emerged with clarity. Never again would I love like that. Never again *could* I love like that.

Once, in Washington, D.C., I'd houseguested with a public relations lady whose Yorkie was ailing. And subject to confusions. Age had come upon Tuffy. Tuffy of the sweet precious face would pad into a corner and remain there. Couldn't leave that spot. Didn't know how to get away from those right-angle walls confronting him. Tuffy would simply stand there endlessly if someone did not turn him about and head him in another direction.

But Tuffy had reached nineteen years. He was entitled to our ministrations and whatever he needed. I was thinking, he had lived a good long loved life. I was thinking, Jazzy would never have the chance to grow old.

Throughout this entire episode I remained a lady. I never screamed. I never accused. However, still nagging at me all this time later is that I never heard from those caregivers who were *supposedly* caring for him after that first twenty-four hours. I understand they didn't know what to say. But when you're handed an adored and well-known healthy dog and you hand back a bloodied dead one, somehow something needs to be said. If you can't handle it in person, do it on the phone. If you can't stomach the phone, there's always a note, a card, flowers, a photo of Jazzy with, maybe, a scrawled "We loved him, too." A message passed through a mutual friend. Something. There needs to be something. There was nothing.

To this day I have never heard one word from them.

There is no way to ever know for absolute sure what happened, and it's not a case to be satisfied via recourse. Money or courts won't give me back Jazzy.

The night I lost Jazzy I stayed alone. Friends wanted to stay over with me. I couldn't bear it. I didn't want company. I couldn't summon the energy to make conversation. I urgently required being alone to cry my heart out. Even though I hadn't made this public, word spread, and a few friends dropped in unannounced. It was like a wake. In the depths of my despair I had to rustle up a makeshift dinner because they lingered. They politely gave me the routine "Oh, forget about it. This is not a time to think about food. We're not hungry, we just came over so you wouldn't be alone." Right. But the time ticks by, the hour grows late, and they don't want to or don't know how to take their leave. I actually had to dial a Chinese eatery for takeout and I had to set the table and I had to put out place mats and ask who wants white wine, who wants red. I was in the center of a bizarre tribal rite.

For months I couldn't speak about it. I didn't write about it. I wouldn't talk about it. (a) I was not able to handle the pain; (b) I didn't believe my pain needed to be shared by anybody else; and (c) I did not want mail sacks from around the world with sad tales of others' own dear departed Fluffys or Fidos.

But the news leaked out. Adding to my anguish, Yorkshire terrier chat rooms began suggesting I must be hiding something, speculating something terrible had obviously happened when Jazzy was in my care "instead of being with a professional handler or in a kennel."

As the press surreptitiously began reporting Jazzy's death, letters came from all over asking what happened. Many had read *The Gift of Jazzy*. I hadn't realized the darling sweet creature who brought a smile to my heart would actually have entered the national consciousness. I simply was not prepared for the outpouring of interest in the little dog I loved so much.

Flowers came, handwritten notes came. Strangers sent yellowed snapshots of their own pets who had gone on with messages telling me to be strong. One note from Tad Smith, an executive of the show-business daily *Variety*, said in part:

> I was so sorry to hear of your tragic loss. Your writing radiates such pluck and sparkle that it is all too easy to forget that even Cindy Adams relies on others for love and support.

Cindy Adams is just like everyone else. A gossip columnist is gift-wrapped as brittle, caustic, smart-mouthed. Maybe true. But take away the sassy brassy reportage about what Pamela Anderson is doing or, better still, who Pamela Anderson is doing, and she's like anyone else.

Friends tore out that day's *New York Post* horoscope. It said:

> If you are in need of help, you will get it, but it may not arrive until the last possible moment. Part of the reason is that your immense Taurus pride prevents you from asking for help, or even looking as if you need it, so people assume you are always on top of your game. It might be an idea to show your more human side today.

The horoscope was correct, I did have to show my human side. And I had to show it immediately. I suddenly had another problem on my hands.

Juicy was my newest problem.

Juicy was going downhill.

In the surrounding tumult, no one had looked after her feelings. She'd taken in the whole drama. She'd seen strangers rushing about, carrying Jazzy, poking him with fearsome needles, feeding him with some strange dripping bottle. She'd been smelling things that were sterile and antiseptic. In all this heightened busyness, she wasn't being noticed or cared for. She wasn't seeing happiness and light-heartedness. She was seeing blood and tension. And then she saw death. She saw him cold. Lifeless. And then she saw him taken away. And then she saw me crying. And then she never saw him again.

Juicy wasn't eating. She wasn't drinking. She wasn't barking. She wasn't engaging. She was frighteningly still and silent. In the deafening quiet of the vet's Emergency waiting room, I suddenly noticed her bunched in someone's arms. It was as though she was asleep. She wasn't moving. Her eyes were focused downward. There wasn't even a whimper.

We offered her food. She didn't take it. We tried to give her water. She wasn't having any. I talked to her. She wouldn't respond. I took her in my arms and warmed her. She didn't move.

For three and three-quarters years my attention had been focused on Jazzy. Accepting Jazzy, training Jazzy, feeding Jazzy, making Jazzy happy, shopping for Jazzy, arranging playdates for Jazzy, learning to live with Jazzy, checking the health of Jazzy. I'd made Jazzy famous. I'd opened a clothing line in Jazzy's name. I'd established Jazzy, the Park Avenue Dog, boutiques in Saks Fifth. I was doing QVC with Jazzy products. I was invited places with Jazzy. Invites came addressed: "Cindy and Jazzy Adams." We were a couple.

Years back I did a news story that led me to a woman in the Midwest. I asked exactly who she was. She replied she was so-and-so's wife. I then asked what she herself did, and her answer was that she cooked, cleaned, and did whatever it was she did for her husband. In other words, she had no identity other than being married to Mr. Whoever. In these last years that was how I felt. Forget that I was nodding to Gwyneth, saying hi to Julianne, getting a quote from Bruce, watching De Niro avoid me, reporting on Madonna, or dissing Barbra, it was as if all I was doing these past three and three-quarters years, my real life's work, was watching over Jazzy, tending Jazzy, seeing that Jazzy was happy.

Worry that Jazzy might be alone was the only reason I'd brought in Juicy in the first place. Jazzy, my raison d'être, was now gone. And it appeared as though I was also about to lose Juicy.

She was so tiny, yet she was throwing everything into turmoil. Juicy needed her temperature taken. Not by me. I was too nervous about hurting her. I had to transport her to the vet to take her temperature. Juicy had to go for shots. Not me. I made Nazalene take her. I couldn't deal with them poking her with a needle.

This newest family member was very smart. She viewed me just as one more undog she had to win out over. She knew exactly how to work me. Even when furnishings were moved about, she always knew the spot where she could find her water bowl. I could not understand why she did not have that same radar when it came to the spot where she was to pee.

Training Juicy was becoming my life's work. Place her in a penned area and she would whine. But never ever would this whining stop. Never. Not even to catch her breath. At forty ounces, how big could her voice box be? Even James Gandolfini runs out of energy. Juicy? Not. Never. Not ever did the whimpering stop. Leave her in the safe penned area in the kitchen to try to teach her and tuck yourself to sleep in your bedroom, she'd whimper all night long. Go to sleep, she's whimpering. Get up seven hours later, she's still whimpering.

She'd whimper while she peed. While she pooped, while she ate, while she barked, while she gnawed at her chew stick, while she played. And she kept jumping up on her half-inch-high legs to try to get out of the pen. And she never stopped jumping while she was whimpering. Finally I took her out of the pen. Not because she'd exhausted herself. She'd exhausted *me*!

One day when my frustration was in overdrive I was with a lady who'd won lunch with me in a charity auction. She told me about her German shepherd who'd come from a monastery. She told me how well trained the German shepherd was. He didn't get up unless she got up, didn't walk unless she walked, never ate from the table. Sat when he was told. Pooped when he was told. "He's really well trained. The nuns used to crack him over the knuckles," she said. "You should think about that with *your* dog."

I thought of Juicy, who has less hair on her than is stuck inside my rat-tail comb, and I thought, Yeah, right.

Instead of actually penning Juicy in, I decided to lay newspaper on the floor of my john. I then confined her by securely blocking its doorway with a doggy gate. Minutes later I was talking on the phone when who sauntered into the library? My roommate.

I left my phone call midway to check the doggy gate. It was still jammed in tightly. It was in one piece. It was in place. I couldn't understand what had happened, but clearly, I hadn't done something right. So, since I had to get back to my phone call, I quickly repeated the process. Placed Juicy on the paper, squarely on a picture of Saddam Hussein—I figured if that couldn't help the potty process, nothing could—made sure the doggy gate hadn't developed some hole or break I hadn't noticed, and scooted back to the library.

So did YouKnowWho. Seconds later there she was, directly alongside me, scrambling to get into a potted plant.

Again I put my caller on hold. Again I got up, albeit less swiftly this time, and investigated. What first caught my eye was that she had Done It. Dead center on Saddam Hussein. Oooooh, good girl, I thought.

But then, how had she gotten out? The doggy gate hadn't been moved by a hair. When Jazzy had been placed

in that john, he couldn't push past. The doggy gate was sufficiently substantial to deter him even though he'd
scratched ferociously to get out. He barked, he grrrred, he
was enraged that it was an obstacle, but there he remained.

I looked again. The gate was untouched. Perfect. What
wasn't perfect was me. This was ten at night. I was feeling
slightly queasy. Like poltergeists were afoot or unknown vis-
itors were out and about in my locked apartment.

Juicy was barking like a lunatic, she was tumbling
around like an acrobat, I was losing my mind, and the person at the other end of the phone was disgusted with me
and hung up. In frustration I dragged over a heavy wing
chair and jammed it against her doggy gate and its doorway.

Huffing and puffing, I ultimately collapsed on my sofa
back in the library. Who's standing alongside me? Juicy.

The next morning everyone banded together to solve
the mystery. To keep where I live from turning into a total
kennel, we cordoned off certain areas. A portable doggy
gate was set up in the front hall. It went flush to the floor
and up against a couch. "Juicy can't get through that," said
Nazalene.

"Impossible for Juicy to get past this," said Reggie.

We all went out on our errands. We all came back. Juicy
was eating a leg of the dressing table in my bedroom.

We were wild. We put Juicy back behind the portable
doggy gate in the front hall, and we hid. We watched. There
is a couch built low, maybe two inches off the floor, that
runs the length of the hall. Juicy, who is either double-

jointed or boneless, had flattened herself out like a stingray and snaked the length of the hall *under* the couch. She'd done the same thing to the bathroom doggy gate the night before. Flattened out like a piece of paper and slid *under* it. She reminded me of those limbo dancers from the Caribbean. The bar goes lower, she goes lower.

Things were just not working. The house was a wreck. I always kept my handbag in one special spot on the floor. It was safe there because, after all these years, Jazzy had known not to go into it. Juicy didn't know. Or care. Juicy got into it. She shredded my papers, destroyed my makeup, took everything out and scattered it. She hid my ballpoint pen, buried it someplace like it was a bone. Each time I came home, I hid the bag in a different place. She'd find it every time and decimate it each time. After a while the problem was not that she could *always* locate it but that I could *never* locate it. I moved it so often that one day I was late for an appointment that I couldn't be late for and I could not get out of the house because I could not remember where I'd stashed my damn purse.

I woke up one night in pain. Juicy had deposited her chew stick under the covers. I turned over in my sleep, and this sharply chewed stick pierced one of my really tender areas. She was on a mission to destroy me as I slept. One weary evening following a very long day, I threw myself in bed dead. Hours later I switched positions and turned my mouth to one side. Something made me wake with a start. My lips had clamped onto an icky yucky slobbery plush toy that had earlier been thrown into some muddy puddle and that this dog now had seen fit to deposit right on my pillow. I let out a shriek and Juicy disappeared. How that cruddy thing got there I don't know. How she got it there I don't know. How she herself had gotten there I didn't know until I peered down. All around the bed it looked like a war zone. Sandbag hell. Nazalene had piled pillows on top of pillows so Juicy could scamper up and down and not hurt herself.

Juicy had been the solo dog In Residence for about a month when I got up especially early to do some work. She was on my bed. I was in another room. She'd suddenly found her voice. No more whining. She barked and barked. Big time she barked. I was terrified. I thought God knows what had happened. I came racing in. Her rubber bone had fallen. Sitting upright, smack on my pillow, she was peering down at the bone, then she stared at me, then she looked again at the bone, then she looked at me. This bitch had summoned me from two rooms away to pick up her bone. And I picked it up.

As far as our relationship was concerned, she was house-breaking me!

Juicy needed to get accustomed to the sounds of the city, so we put her on the terrace. She liked the terrace. She got so she'd stand at its glass door. Just stand there and bark and bark until someone opened it or I went out of my mind. But she wouldn't stay outside by herself. Once out there, she'd howl until someone came to keep her company.

On a warm easy lazy afternoon, we'd drag out her comfy

faux fur bed and plop it down right in a sunny patch so she could sun herself. We'd bring treats. We'd fetch water. We'd scramble back and forth for her favorite toys. Forget it. Once out there alone, she wanted no part of a terrace that real estate brokers would die for. We'd take her downstairs for a few minutes at a time to get her used to the cabs honking and brakes screeching. Five steps from our building she'd lie right down in the patch of sun she found right in the gutter right in the middle of the avenue right in the middle of the cabs and buses that were now honking because of her as they jammed on their brakes that were now screeching because of her.

As the weather turned to fall, I bought Juicy a wardrobe of sweaters—extra small—with little legs in them. With a tape measure I measured her neck. Six inches. I measured her waist. I measured neck to tail. Nothing was small enough. I was so concerned about hurting her and twisting those four skinny pipe stems to thread them into the little holes that, rather than pull her, I pulled the sweater. Acrylic or cashmere, the garments became more accessible, but by then they were stretched. The looser they got the more they hung underneath. They were like hammocks bubbling under that teeny belly.

One saleslady showed me a $160 quilted coat, 100 percent double-thick, cable-knit virgin wool with extra-long turtleneck that could be folded in half plus hood, arm cuffs, leg straps, and Velcro undersection. I said, "Hon, this isn't some aging whippet warding off a blustery winter in the woods of Oregon. I'm looking for a chenille Band-Aid."

I checked seventy-five different styles, including one designed to look like the front page of a newspaper. No matter how we redid them, resewed them, rejiggered them, and readjusted them, they wouldn't work. Time after time Juicy fell flat. She tripped. She stumbled. She tumbled. Her legs kept wriggling out of the wool. They were too short to stay inside. Also she got cranky waiting while I tried stuffing them through the openings. Then the bulky part that covered her stomach got in the way of whatever it shouldn't get in the way of. I couldn't believe it. My beautiful brand-new daughter not a fashion statement? I mean, please.

As Juicy crept into my bones, I began to disappear by the part. First I had lost my heart. Then I started losing my mind.

The night I had to cover the Tony Awards I was wearing Armani. I'd tracked the outfit for months. I'd waited until it got to the Woodbury Common outlet, which is a markdown center in upstate New York. It's like a whole discount village of Armanis, Escadas, Chanels, Calvins. Up there my suit was 30 off. In addition, I'd taken back a handbag somebody gave me. I liked the bag but I needed the suit more, so I put the credit toward it. In actual cash, the suit ended up costing me less than 50 percent of its regular price. The problem was, it was such a long drive there and took so much in gas that I nearly blew what I saved in the sale.

Anyway, this particular night I was backstage and working the red carpet arrivals. I bantered with Hugh Jackman, tried to look through Sarah Jessica Parker's see-through Gucci, interacted with Melanie Griffith, who looked nifty even in broad daylight with little makeup on, and talked to Antonio Banderas, who told me: "When I did the musical *Nine* on Broadway, it was hard. Maybe for others this difficult art form is easier. For me doing twelve songs a night was very demanding. I lived only for these two and a half hours a night. I spoke just to my wife, my babies, and my personal assistant when I was not working. I tried to save my voice. And I didn't even go out after the performance. I had to save the energy. I just went back home, where I made some little snack for myself."

I realized I had finally and forever lost my marbles when, rather than rub shoulders and notebooks with glossy celebrities like Edie Falco and Billy Joel, I wanted nothing more than to rush home and lay my sale-priced-Armani-covered body on my kitchen floor and suck the fluffy raggy little ear of Juicy. Rub Juicy's infinitesimal patent-leather nose. Chew the ends of Juicy's Confucius-style mustache. Put my face on her little face and kiss it. And that's what I did. There were lines around the block at Radio City Music Hall. There were metal detectors and guards and security passes to get close. And I, with my assigned seat in the orchestra, raced home to cuddle my only child.

Juicy has a face a magazine illustrator would draw. My neighbors couldn't keep their hands off her. Parade her on the street in the sparkly maribou ensemble I'd had made for her and grown men got to their knees on the sidewalk, little old ladies with their walkers bent down, cabdrivers slowed to smile. Even in busy high-rise buildings, New Yorkers rarely know who lives near them. No time to pass the time of day. They're too busy surviving. Suddenly, faces I'd never noticed before were coming out of the woodwork.

A gossip column breeds a busy environment. Phones ringing. Messengers and FedExes and packages arriving. Coming in steadily are releases, invites, reminders, memos, items, announcements of new eateries that close before you get there, unwanted bios and résumés and photos, requests to send used shoes or torn socks or whatever as part of those endless celebrity auctions for esoteric charities like The Care and Feeding of the Endangered White Rhino of Downtown Tanzania. Maybe because our values today are skewed, maybe because it seems manners have taken a hike, whatever the reason—gossip is a hot commodity. Costing nothing, it's a ticket to another life. Gossip is a cheap, quick fix. As long as you have that column, someone always wants you to grace some function. The mail is so heavy that often I don't open it for a week. There's an impersonal insatiable gnawing hunger out there. You are wanted not for yourself but to feed the starving egos of the world.

I know it's not me personally. I know the minute I have no byline I'll be home alone, scavenging for some dry rusk to gnaw for dinner. I learned this at the feet of Barbara Bush, who was then First Lady. At the end of a meaningful conversation, the wife of the elder President George Bush said: "The simple fact is, George is now in office. He's *in*. And when the time comes that he's out, we'll both be out. That's the way Washington, D.C., works. George and I expect that. We've been around too long. We've seen it happen many times before to our friends. They get dropped from all the party lists. And so will I. And so will he. That's part of political life, and I'm prepared for it."

Then she let out a hoot of a laugh. She said, "You and I are realistic enough to understand that. We can't be kidded. I mean, we're pros."

The truth is, the higher you go, the less anyone really knows you—and the more you need that pure simple love of an animal who won't care if you're in the White House, the doghouse, or the big house.

Today, everyone every place is busy. But the busiest of the busy is New York, the capital of the world. New Yorkers are always rushing. Where I live is a little island on which the whole entire immediate-known universe is hustling deals. New Yorkers don't walk, they run. It's joggers trying to keep their figure, pedestrians trying to keep their wallets, tourists who, despite our gridlocked crosswalk signs that say no standing, no stopping, no parking, no kidding, know jaywalking is faster than a cab. They're all in a hurry.

And all lugging. New York's next generation will be permanently shaped like Quasimodo. We're all lugging tote bags. Survival kits. Some of us drag two. The regular large-size purse, which could take us round the world and has gym shoes, office shoes, and since there's no time to go home and change, the evening makeup, jewelry, and cocktail purse. Plus our office bag, which has the day's inventory, files, beeper, Filofax, schedules, pad, pencil, tape recorder, phone log, address book, lunch, best seller we're looking to read, magazine we intend to read, newspaper we're supposed to read, and that omnipresent bottle of water, which today nobody leaves home without any more than they'd go without underarm spray. We professional New York ladies don't need dates. We need redcaps.

The town is so busy it has no time for anything. What's done with all this time saved, I don't know, but it's Minute rice, instant coffee, short-order cooks, quick fix, fast food, Jiffy Lube, one-stop shopping. It's multitasking. Working the BlackBerry while on a bus while talking to a colleague while dialing the cell to order takeout.

New York is Attitude City. Home plate for such one-namers as Rosie, Rudy, Ricki, Whoopi, Woody, Sally, Halle, Maury, Connie, Christie, Conan, Calvin, Dustin, Quentin, Yoko, Geraldo, Mira, Nicole, Julia, Meg, Bruce, and even Ashton.

Where else do you get Letterman, Cosby, and Imus in one town? Where else can you wait in line for the john next to Kissinger, catch Zellweger in a restaurant, watch Pacino being chauffeured in his Jeep, see Harrison and Calista arm in arm, sit with Roy Scheider at Starbucks, stand behind Bacall getting takeout at a deli.

And in the center of this maelstrom is its juicy tabloid, the *New York Post*. And in the middle of this newspaper is—

me. I write a gossip column for it six days a week. And my private office in my home is the eye of my storm. And into this hurricane environment—with phones ringing, faxes, e-mails, IMs, hand deliveries, doorbells announcing yet another mail drop from the paper, techies coming and going fixing computers, interviews and meetings and real live people for lunch/tea/dinner/breakfast/snacks—what was not needed was a dog with an attitude problem.

Take Juicy's first party. Long before we lost Jazzy, I'd committed to giving a buffet dinner for Gene Simmons of Kiss. Understand, Gene Simmons of Kiss and I had never met. Nor was he ecstatic about rectifying the situation. To him I was a Cro-Magnon.

Gene had contracted for a series of memoirs. Publisher Michael Viner understood the juxtaposition of me—who considers Frank Sinatra still cutting edge musicwise—and Gene Simmons—whose bio admits he's bedded over 1,000 nubile maidens—to be a PR match made in heaven. Michael wanted to hustle Gene's book *Sex Money Kiss* to a new non-Kiss audience and gave Gene a choice. Either do *Sesame Street* or do Cindy's press party. Reluctantly, he picked me.

A party for rock 'n' rollers is culture shock for a baby dog. Even for an old one, like me. I didn't send Juicy away, because shipping her off to another strange haven might've been traumatic at this point. A problem was, feet and legs belonging to caterers were traipsing through Juicy's new world. Stiletto heels and lickable naked toes were clumping around this tiny body. Strangers whom I didn't know and who definitely hadn't yet made Juicy's acquaintance were throughout. While I was warning everyone to look out for her, I myself fell over her. We cleared a safe spot under a kitchen banquette, only to have a delivery boy slide in a carton of white wine that came to rest a hair away from her tail. I picked her up, kissed her, and said, "Juicy Adams, welcome to the hood."

Juicy and I had a problem. We both wanted to be boss. I did a TV show with her. It was embarrassing. Here I was promoting my dog, selling my dog—my dog this, my dog that, how my dog and I love each other—and no matter what I wanted her to do, she wouldn't do it. Sit quietly in Mommy's lap while Mommy's telling her long-winded tiresome anecdote that they'd already requested and had B-roll footage to go with? No. That was when she'd upstage me, jump up and lick off all my lipstick so nobody paid attention to this brilliantly rehearsed anecdote. Another time, when I was running out of steam and hadn't anything more to say, it was show-and-tell time. Kiss Mommy. Show the world how you love Mommy. In other words, kiss off the lipstick *now*, you rotten dog. No. Nothing. She'd lie motionless, flat on my lap like a sphinx.

I missed Jazzy. Outwardly, I'd try to dismiss it breezily with "Hey, everyone plays the hand they're dealt." But inwardly, what I was wondering was, What had I done that I was getting punished? If God was good, why was I in such emotional pain?

The oddities of my life were achingly evident at this point. On the one hand, I was complaining about God, on the other, I was writing about God. When this descended on me, I'd been prepping a piece about what might have happened if down that yellow brick road to 1600 Pennsylvania Avenue came Senator Joe Lieberman, an Orthodox Jew. I'd had an exclusive that Hadassah Lieberman told someone that, were her husband ever elected, she would make the White House kosher. Purer than just kosher. Her exact words were "I would definitely keep the White House Glatt kosher."

Glatt kosher means super kosher. Besides no pork, ham, shellfish, it checks the cuts of meat and signifies even the veggies have been pronounced clean. It means food examined and certified worthy by two independent rabbis. Rules require two kitchens. Two dishwashers. Two everything— dishes, silver, pots, pans. One for meat. One for dairy. Two sets of your everyday cheapo stuff, and two of the expensive state banquet jobs. Plus a whole special Passover set. All of which would extend to Air Force One and Camp David.

I ended with "State guests would be able to enjoy Hadassah's pot roast. They would not, however, be able to splash milk—skim, whole, half-and-half, cream, whatever—into their dinner beverage. It'll be soy milk. As in soy vey."

Even I had to smile at that. I was coming out of my dark tunnel.

Periodically, black thoughts came knocking at the door of my consciousness: I should have spared extra time for playing with him. Maybe worked a little less, maybe walked with him a little more. Maybe cherished him even when he was a bad dog and used my couch for a men's room . . .

These furry fluffy beings are an alone person's support system. They make you smile, they make your eyes crinkle up when life's blows could have made them turn down. They are Divine Love's angels on this side of the veil.

Juicy had stopped looking in all Jazzy's favorite spots for him. Juicy was now claiming her rightful place in the center of my lap.

I took a deep breath. Life is good. Life goes on.

FIVE

Get Out and Party

My makeup artist, Anne-Marie Oliver—
she's unmarried but hunting—said to me:
"I can't find anyone who passes my toilet
bowl test."

"Your what?" I asked as I examined
my labial folds, those lines that run from the sides of your
nose to the chin.

"My toilet bowl test is 100 percent accurate," she said,
rubbing in a now heavier concealer.

"What's the test?"

"I have a rule. Nobody uses my toilet. Say a telephone
repair guy, a cable maintenance man, a first-time date comes
to my apartment. Say he needs to use my bathroom. I let
nobody in there. I tell them the thing's broken and I'm
waiting for the plumber. The only time any man ever uses
my john is when he's my type. Not my type, he can shake it

behind a tree for all I care—he doesn't make my personal bathroom."

I was beginning to think, Hey, right, it's time to party. Time for me to maybe find a guy who could pass the toilet bowl test.

That afternoon I was chauffeuring Juicy to the country. She was having a playdate with a Maltese named Raffles. Being a city person, I couldn't find my way. I don't understand directions that start "At a bent elm tree turn left." So I was lost. I leaned out and called to a farmer. He didn't hear me. He shouted back, "Eh? Can you repeat that, missus?" *Missus?* From far away he could tell that I was no longer a plain *miss?* I right away knew the time for me was growing short.

When I finally arrived, I watched the little boy Raffles try to play Romeo to my juicy Juliet. The playdate's mother murmured, "Could be she needs a little sex." I thought to myself, Sounds good to me.

Enter Darryl. A CEO in the hotel business. His company kept him traveling coast to coast. That was the good part. Not the part about him seeing the country on a regular basis. The part about me seeing him on an irregular basis. I liked that Darryl was a part-timer. Every other weekend was perfect. I can understand taking a man for richer or poorer. But for lunch? Any guy hanging around to watch me fold bananas into the Jell-O every single Sunday does not fit my idea of *House Beautiful.*

Dr. Joyce Brothers told me that CEOs are programmed to be competitive and aggressive, and they're winners, *but* "they leave it all in the office. Too much coffee during the day, too much martini at lunch, too much Bufferin at night makes for too little anything else. They get their stroking with barbers, tailors, and masseurs. With the brain the most powerful sexual instrument of all, after a tense day theirs are worn out."

Well, maybe. But this CEO's other various parts were A-OK. Take, for instance, his wallet. The man was a born-again Santa. When he bought me toys, it was at Tiffany "R" Us. And when he sent flowers, it was like for a gangster's funeral. I have a hard time finding generosity a flaw.

There was only one tiny thing I didn't love enormously. He was a little bit of an egotist. Just a little bit. A very little bit. The problem was, we were both attracted to him. Handsome Darryl, with hair that was lush Grecian Formula brown, was tall, dark, and narcissistic. The biweekly visit to his barber was a main event. He'd ask, "Should I get the sides trimmed? What do you think?" I'd think, What I think is you should get a life.

His idea of giving me a treat was to allow me to accompany him to his tailor, where we'd all stand in the mirror and admire him. The tailor would drape a canvas in pins on his perfectly proportioned five-eleven-and-three-quarters frame. He'd squint into the mirror and pirouette around slowly. The tailor would squint into the mirror and walk around slowly.

"You have to rotate the sleeve," Darryl would say.

"Ahaaa, absolutely. Rotate the sleeve," the tailor would parrot.

"Christ, yes. I mean, my God, rotate that damn sleeve," I would say.

He said one evening, "We have to have a serious talk."

Uh-oh, I thought. Serious? He's looking to get serious? I didn't want to get serious. A guy who's better looking than I am just doesn't do it for me. I figured I'd find a way to let him down gently.

"Look, we need a serious talk," he repeated.

I knew he wouldn't get down on bended knee because it might crease the pants, but . . . ugh . . . here it comes . . . the proposal. "Go ahead, what do you want to say?" I said. "Say it."

"I don't do dogs," he said.

"You don't do dogs?" I repeated inanely.

"No. I like them. I just don't have anything to do with them. I'm not into dogs. They're unclean. They take too much effort."

Juicy at that moment was into some heavy-duty licking of my lids. She views my lids with the same enthusiasm Jackie Mason would view a pastrami on rye. "Have you always lived dogless?"

"Well, yes. And I don't know how to tell you this, but I'm not really comfortable around dogs. They don't always behave."

Juicy had moved on to my nose. "So what would you suggest I do? Send Juicy away to military school?"

"No. I just wondered if there was some alternative."

Yes, I thought, and you're *it*. Was this guy for real? Get rid of Juicy? Better to get rid of *him*—and the eighteen-millimeter black Tahitian pearl ring he'd given me for my birthday. Well, maybe not better, but . . . I began to think I'd send back the ring. Just the ring. I sort of thought maybe I'd keep the pearl.

"I mean," he said, "watching your little dog kissing you on the mouth is . . . I mean . . . it's like . . . well, it really isn't sanitary."

"Really? Two Cubans in heat transmit more bacilli between them than my pampered Yorkie ever could."

At this point Juicy skittered past one sleeve that had just been rotated. Darryl extended his hand stiffly to pat the dog the same way a disciplinarian might tap the head of a kindergarten child who'd just been chastised, then told, "Very well, now go out and play, there's a good boy."

They say a horse knows if a rider's afraid of it. It has to do with pheromones or something. I don't know exactly how, but I knew Juicy knew. She knew who loved her and who didn't. After this ceremonial pat on her head, my sweet Yorkshire terrier walked around and around. I watched as Juicy's two-and-a-half-pound body made a complete circle, then sat down with her rear toward Darryl and her tiny docked tail pointing straight at his face. She wasn't giving him the finger, she was giving him the rump. In Castilian Dogese she was telling him: "Kiss my ass."

I reached out for a hug—we're talking Juicy, not Darryl—and the two-legged one said, "You're like a kid. If it's just something you want to pet, I'll get you a stuffed toy."

I said, "I do not want a stuffed toy. A stuffed toy is inert. Juicy is ert."

The phone rang. It was Her Ertness Shirley MacLaine, who is also having a love affair with her dog. She said to me, "Terry is royal."

"Excuuuuse me," said I, "but you're talking about a rat terrier. Rat terriers are *royal?*"

"She's truly some princess I once knew in Egypt. I have nine other dogs on my ranch in New Mexico, but they're not indoor dogs. And the other nine know she's royalty."

"Yeah? So why'd you need a tenth dog?"

"For the mice. I tried cats, but the outdoor dogs did in the cats. I saw this one in a pet shop, and I had a premonition—especially when I heard she's a rat terrier."

Peering sideways at Darryl, I said, "So, Shirl, how indoor is she? Like, does she sleep with you?"

"Of course. What kind of a question is that? Certainly. In my bed. In my arms or wherever else she decides."

I asked Shirley what if she found another man in her life. She said, "Well, they'd just have to learn their place." Who, the dog? "No, the guy. He'd have to see that Terry's place is right in bed with me, under my arm. A new man would just have to understand the pecking order. There are priorities, and he'd have to know she's staying right there. Terry isn't going to leave my bed just for him. Terry would sleep between us."

I didn't yet know what to do about my own place cards. It was enough for Juicy that this interloper was anywhere in the house. My sweet dog tore the guest room to shreds. Darryl's towel was torn, his newspaper shredded, his clothes—even with the newly rotated sleeve—got chewed. Viewing the mayhem, I let out a shriek. Juicy knew perfectly well what she'd done. She ran like hell and hid under a table.

The atmosphere wasn't improved the next morning, when my houseguest's first sound was "Coffee? Somebody going to make coffee?"

"What do you mean 'somebody'? I'm the only somebody here."

Fifteen minutes later, as that heavenly aroma began wafting guest-roomward, he said: "Maybe better decaf. They say you shouldn't have too much coffee."

"Who's 'they'? Right now I am the they who is making this coffee."

I padded across the whole apartment to transport the cup to him. Once I crossed that divide again and was back in the kitchen came the voice calling: "Cold. It's cold. The coffee's cold."

"Why didn't you drink it when I first brought it in?"

"It was too hot."

I delivered a fresh cup. He reached for it without looking. He knocked it over. It stained the carpet. I was now cleaning the carpet, and he still needed coffee.

Between his two cups and my one cup, I depleted my small pot. He said, "I have a great idea. How about a cozy Sunday breakfast for two? Just us. Why don't you just whip up something?"

"Whip what? What something?"

"Anything."

"Like what anything?"

"Nothing special. Just breakfast. Bagels, cream cheese, a little grapefruit juice. I feel like grapefruit juice. Listen, bacon and eggs would be nice if you have it. If not, okay. I don't want you to go to any trouble. And not a lot. I don't want a lot. Just a little."

"I don't have bagels in the house. Yogurt I have. Also berries."

He stared as if seeing me for the first time. "No bagels? What do you mean you don't have bagels? Neil Sedaka says his house always has bagels."

"So go to Neil Sedaka's house."

"A house with no bagels? I never heard such a thing."

While he was acting as if I lived in some desolate cave in Afghanistan, I discovered Juicy had gotten her paws and whiskers into a little strawberry jam. I stuck Juicy in the kitchen sink, doused her with warm water spray, added a natural herbal shampoo, then Keri lotion, then accompanied by lots of kisses, lifted her onto a thick dry towel and plugged in my hair dryer. At this moment Darryl, who'd buttoned himself into his slightly chewed suit in order to run down for a desperately needed bagel, was crossing the kitchen heading for the back door. Exactly as he sauntered past, Juicy treated herself to one wild vigorous massive shake. A drowned Saint Bernard wouldn't have given off more water. Darryl's suit—with the rotated sleeve—was drenched.

And thus ended my shot at my future husband the CEO.

I prepared to go back into the dating mode. The problem was, who had the energy for what it took? I'd read somewhere—maybe even in my own column—that Liz Hurley used Donatella Versace's special olive oil just to take stretch marks out of her belly. Assuming you're stretch mark–less, you also need breath mints, pedicure, waxing, exfoliation so your skin's not soft only where it shows in polite company, and the superskinnysexysilky negligee that reveals more than an MRI.

It's creaming your everything—from elbows to scaly feet. A dermatologist suggested glycolic lotion for rubbing into what's called your laugh lines. Those are the lines that are laughing even when you're not. It's going to sleep with so much gook that you slip out of bed.

And collagen? You can get so pumped that if you fall down you'll bounce. Or look like Cher's lips. Dentists say to floss in the morning, after breakfast, before lunch, instead of tea, following dinner, during your late night cookie fix, and before bed. I was so busy flossing I didn't have time to eat.

My hairdresser says spraying is not good. This I know. I don't have to pay sixty-five dollars for a wash and set to hear that. She says to brush a hundred strokes every night. The maintenance is such that I'm beginning to think bald is not so bad. At least it's neat.

The pedicurist says callus removal requires a pumice stone to buff the soles twice a day. My cosmetologist says to strengthen lashes she advises schmearing with Vaseline. If I did that I couldn't open my eyes wide enough to find the floss for the teeth, the brush for the hair, or the pumice for my soles.

Tova Borgnine says to prevent turning into an alligator handbag, you must use her Tova Nine face mask, the one her husband, Ernest Borgnine, uses. I mean, I love Ernie, but Julia Roberts he's not. My manicurist frets over my cuticles. "They're getting raggedy," she says. I say, "You would, too, if you had to do this much work on yourself."

Some physiotherapist prescribed butt-tightening exercises to get rid of any valance beneath the cheeks. Forty-five minutes every morning. Who has forty-five minutes in the morning? That's when you're creaming, massaging, flossing, and Vaselining.

A masseur told me to oil my whole body every day. However, he swears this won't take extra time because I can do it while I'm tightening my bum. There's also hoisting the legs against a wall, propping them on pillows, or splashing shower water onto them to unpuff the veins. There's also sleeping with gloves so glycerin can drench the cracked, dry hands.

They say if you don't do all of this, you won't stay stunning enough to date. I say if you do all of this, you won't have *TIME* to date.

To check out the newest female hygiene merchandise, I went to a drugstore in my area. At the cashier's desk, a richly dressed tall guy was locked in mortal combat. A cranky computer had rejected his unlimited AmEx card, and the salesladies were crowded around eyeing him unblinkingly.

This tall fellow, irritated beyond belief, was tapping his foot and muttering, "But it's a VIP card. There's no limit to what I can charge. What do you mean it's rejecting my purchase? That's impossible."

I wriggled myself next to him.

Donald Sutherland!

I had history with Donald Sutherland. We'd been dais mates shortly before at a black-tie event. Sutherland had flown from California especially for that event. His plane had been late. His car had sprung a leak. His formal Armani threads had accidentally become mix 'n' match. And he was upset. "My secretary packed my last year's tuxedo jacket with the trousers of my tailcoat," a perspiring, anguished Donald had told me as he sat in a blue tux jacket with black tuxedo pants. I ran my hands over him. The fabrics felt the same. "But the *colors* are *different*," he whispered hoarsely.

And now, only a few months later, a stupid machine had sent his eighty-seven dollars' worth of shampoo and soap down the drain. An angry Donald, frustrated in this drugstore with everyone watching him being rejected by a machine, wheeled around, only to come face-to-face with GuessWho. Staring right into my eyes, he growled, "You! You're bad luck for me."

Outside, in the rainy street, he couldn't get a taxi. He probably blamed me for that, too.

I managed to get out of there and home because I was due to go to a movie with my next future ex-beau. This go-to-the-movies pal is a male model. He has an Irish face, curly red hair, green eyes, is six-foot-one, 170 pounds, has a thirty-three waist with inseam to match, and looks great in wardrobe.

Gay guys make terrific walkers. A walker is someone harmless enough to be acceptable to a husband as an escort for his wife when he's unavailable. A walker dresses well, possesses social know-how, makes no romantic demands, usually has no money, but if he's studly-looking enough, can pass for the real thing enough to make others wonder how you shanghaied such a hotshot catch. Walkers—on whose arms you walk into a room—are especially useful for black-tie invitations that come addressed "And Guest." They're the Guest. And if they have a car, even better.

Chad was into major gossip. He knew which lady models were doing coke and which male models were doing male models. The conversation was never boring. He understood the price to pay to be a repeat guest at a New York dinner party. The currency is whatever tidbit you bring to the table. The result was he was always entertaining. And valuable. These types handle the minutiae of your life. They arrange the appointments, make the reservations, argue with the caterer. They know where to shop for a discount, what photographer to get for your photo shoot, and that you don't wear horizontal stripes unless you're the width of Calista Flockhart.

If, for instance, he was there as I finished my last-minute accessorizing, it went something like this:

"*What?* You're going to wear that bag with that gown?"

"Yes."

"Please. Don't tell me that."

"Why, what's wrong with it?"

"Are you crazy? You some kind of nut? They'll laugh at you. Nobody wears that kind of a bag with that kind of a gown."

"But I like it."

"Please. Just thank God I'm here to help you."

Back goes the bag. He selects another one.

With him the world was easier. It was like frozen pizza. It all came ready-made. Homosexuals don't have to get in touch with the lady's feminine side. They *are* the feminine side. It's comfortable. Chad and I began to hang out together. I knew the worst that could happen was he'd cheat with an Eagle Scout.

He lived two blocks away. And he was helpful where the

true love of my life was concerned. Vets advise knocking your dogs out once a year so they have the proper dental hygiene. But Juicy was too little so Chad found me a pet toothpaste that tastes and smells like peanut butter. I could put it on my finger, and it worked. She could have posed for Ipana.

One hot summer weekend I had to be away and boarded Juicy with Chad. His studio was in a brownstone. The only neighbor on his floor was an elderly spinster who had a garden apartment. Despite the fact that his sleepover guest had pointy ears and a docked tail, Chad cracked his door to catch a bit of air. Juicy Adams nudged it open, and out she skipped. She clambered onto the neighbor's small rock sculpture and in through her open window. The lady was out for the evening. About ten-fifteen the air was rent with piercing screams. Coming home, unbolting her padlocked door, the lady had gone into the bedroom. There she found a ferocious Yorkshire terrier on the pillow, calmly licking her undersection.

Chad gave Juicy attention. I loved that. In return he got Juicy's attention. I didn't love that. For instance, he was feeding her chicken. When next I fed her dog food, she dissed me. I finally tore up small bits of boneless skinless freshly boiled white chicken breast direct from the pot. She looked at it, looked at me, and went after Chad again. I didn't get it. He didn't cootchy-coo her and play games like Paws Pause—putting both your hands on both front paws and when the dog pulls away you do it again and place her paws atop your hands and then pull out your hands and put them on top of her paws and on and on. I did this. I loved her madly and couldn't understand her behavior.

Eventually I unraveled the mystery. I'd been serving white meat. Chad had been feeding her dark meat. My dog preferred the dark. I changed the menu and got my dog back.

Chad and I enriched each other's lives. We still do. However, although we still share the movies, fashion tips, and everyone's secrets, I did not see us celebrating the Big Day together. I mean, which of us would be the bride?

I had an epiphany one morning. I realized I was content. Happy, in fact. It was actually a good time in my life. I had a coterie of male buddies who were around for me, and because I wasn't tied up with a husband or steady escort, I had the best of both worlds. I could also enjoy time with this planet's most interesting women, many of whom are my best friends.

Once a month Barbara Walters and I have a quiet just-us dinner. October it's my treat, November it's hers, and so it goes. A month when it was her turn, she said, "Enough with the same places. Let's find something new and trendy."

We arrived, and the welcoming bow was so deep the maître d' bent into a hoop. Escorting us to a prime table that was awaiting us although this new and trendy bistro was jammed, he said, "The chef has prepared a tasting menu for you."

"Thanks, but I'd just like something simple," I said.

"The chef has personally prepared a tasting menu for you," he insisted.

"Well, what's on your tasting menu?" Barbara asked.

"The chef is specializing in game this evening. We're serving deer."

"Please. I can't eat Bambi," I said.

"Also roast suckling pig."

"I don't do pig," Barbara said.

"Also delicately pink duck."

"I'm not into underdone duck." She sighed. "Could we simply order some fish?"

Standing stiffly—the man's spine was obviously armor-plated—he repeated slowly: "The chef has prepared a tasting menu for you."

Because we wanted to toast one another, I just pointed to something sort of familiar on the wine list and asked, "Is that good?"

"Yes," he said. "It's good."

Whatever it was, it went fine with the bread, which was becoming our main dish. In fact, at one point the maître d' said in a snarky voice: "Perhaps you'd eat more of our food if you weren't eating so much bread."

We didn't care. We were so wrapped up in nonstop conversation that we weren't much aware of what was on the table.

At the end Barbara said, "Figures there's no check here because of how they pushed their own tasting menu. I usually tip 20 percent, but if we're not getting any bill, I'm not sure what to do. What should I leave?"

I said, "Ask for the check. Sometimes they give it to you

to sign even when it's complimentary." So she asked. And it came. And it was $950! And they asked for her credit card.

We looked at each other in shock. $950! The wine had been $500!

Because we were just two ladies anxious not to cause any fuss, and because we couldn't figure what else to do, Barbara paid the tab. Plus she added the 20 percent. Plus I was so horrified about picking the stupid place and picking the stupid wine that I sent her a gift the next day. It ended up costing $1,500 for the two of us to eat bread.

We decided that, probably, this would not have happened if we'd been with a man.

The man would have known better than to order blind. He'd have inquired about the price. Or the sommelier would have respected him sufficiently to hint, "This wine is a bit pricey. Might I suggest something else?"

Enter Stan, short for Stansfield. Handsome Stansome I called him. Stan is from Connecticut. A widower, he is also a lawyer. To Stan, every client—including those who are already in prison—is innocent. "Falsely accused" is his precise phrase.

Stansfield loved celebrities. Amongst his clients was a rock 'n' roller who'd given us front-row tickets to a Fleetwood Mac concert. The whole bunch—Stevie Nicks, Mick Fleetwood, John McVie, Lindsey Buckingham—were staying at different hotels. If you phoned, you had to know the alias or you didn't get through. Lindsey's transport was a limo so stretched that it reached New Jersey while still double-parked in New York. I asked what their tour bus was like. He said, "We don't do buses. We have our own 727." Right. Okayyyy.

On the ride out to the arena, Lindsey spoke about his lifestyle: "R 'n' R burns you out in your forties. I used to start my day at seven P.M. and finish with the sun. On the road it was three times crazier." He now lives a "simple" life in his eight-thousand-square-foot Bel Air home and is "working on having friends."

Stan told me: "Wear flats. Go casual." I wore flats. I went casual. The other assorted ladies were into four-inch stiletto boots, beaded jeans so tight they wear out from the inside, scoop-neck sweaters that stopped three inches before their belly buttons, and diamond Judith Ripka necklaces.

We left at 4:30 for the 8:15 concert. Sound check was early because whatever the voodoo she do, Stevie Nicks, who rehearsed with her hair in rollers and who'd brought her two Yorkies, needs three hours to get ready. I asked why. I was told, "She gets a massage." But if you have to get "up" for a performance, wouldn't you want something stimulating, not relaxing? Someone answered: "We don't know. We only know she needs three hours to get ready."

When the slammin' wham-bam concert was over, I was ready to make out a will for my ears, which had gone dead.

After seven hours away from Juicy, I begged off from any more rollicking good time. Unlike Stevie Nicks, I hadn't brought *my* Yorkie, and I had to feed her.

Having heard this one before, Stan said to me, "It's midnight. How many times a day do you feed her? She's not three pounds. How much can she eat?"

Stansfield and I had lots in common. One area of commonality was we were both into careers that required study. I appreciated his lawyerly, orderly mind. He believed that every professional, no matter what his discipline, was enriched by studying law. "Makes your thinking tidy," he says. "Methodical." And he wasn't afraid to date powerful women. Insecure men won't. Or don't. He'd dated a lady COO, a famous artist, a curator. I liked that about him.

We'd visit each other's workplaces. His housed three cats. He'd once had five. Not only did Stan's cats not like dogs, they did not even like Stan's other cats. The fat old tom wouldn't enter the same room as the year-old skinny kitten, while the female Persian burrowed into a closet. I brought my baby over for the families to sort of get to know one another. Stan was jumpy. When Juicy skedaddled across the back of the couch, he leaned around to watch. If she broke left, his eyes went left. His eyes never left Juicy.

The few seconds his irises weren't locked on her, his feet were. His shoes were longer than she, even with her pink tongue out panting in front and tiny tail wagging in back. I told him, "You have to do the Yorkie Shuffle."

"Yorkie Shuffle?"

"Slide along the floor. That way you won't step on her."

Juicy's so small she somehow always ended up *under* his 13-D boot. We tried hanging a bell on her. It didn't work. Her bell made more noise than she did.

The moment came to introduce his four-legged Hatfields to my McCoy. My pooch immediately helped herself to the tom's litter box and ate his food. Friendly Juicy, who just wanted a pal, jumped around, eager to play. The tom jumped too. But not around Juicy. *At* her. Hissing. Back arched. Claws and paws extended, ready to rake her. Panicked, I snatched up my child a heartbeat before the tom made her into Juicyburgers.

I managed to sidestep the Persian who crept out of her closet to see what the ruckus was about, but who accounted for an appendage the size of a feather duster! Yorkie tails are docked. The average thumb is longer. I thus did not allow for a Persian's long and lush bushy tail. I tripped over it and, in trying to pivot around her body, fell down smack on top of her. Miss Persian let out a piercing scream. Animal-wise, things were not going well with us.

Stansfield subsequently came to the *New York Post*. It was a day Oscar-winning director Ron Howard was making a drop-in. Ron loved the *Post's* can. He'd actually researched it for his movie *The Paper*, which featured a scene where the editor called for the pressroom chief, who could not respond because, per the script, he was answering a call of nature.

The day Stansfield came Ron was reminiscing: "We deliberately picked this *New York Post* john for our scene."

I glanced at my dog. I couldn't let Juicy sniff around this prizewinning toilet or romp untethered through the newsroom, where her species was definitely not allowed. I fretted about the piles of newspaper atop every desk, computer, chair, and inch of floor. My dogs were trained on newspaper, so in their view it existed for only one purpose. Not wanting to take any chances, I zipped her into her carrier and joined Ron back inside the men's room.

This bathroom extraordinaire had double sinks and six stalls. The sinks were stained, the rubber floor runner studded with cigarette butts, and the urinals featured wadded, wet paper towels atop them. The stalls had the discount version of Charmin trailing the floor. We are not talking *Harper's Bazaar* here.

Ron was saying: "The john we built on the set wasn't right. Too small. I personally inspected other toilets around, and there was not enough . . . er . . . atmosphere."

"Like not crappy enough?"

He grinned. "We decided we'd keep this exactly as we found it. No changes."

A pause, then Ron added: "You people have a really great can here."

I puffed with pride. To think that of all the powder rooms possible, our pressroom sanctuary had the crappiest this big-time moviemaker could find. Sic transit Alexander Hamilton.

Once unzipped, Juicy did her usual number. Stretched out her front legs full length, stretched out her back paws full length, then rolled all over the floor, rubbing, scratching, and massaging herself. Then, being a trashy type, she lay flat out on her back. Then sat down, erect, head high, face out, ears straight up like antennae, eyes staring unblinkingly at me, just waiting to be adored. All the while Stan struggled to understand what he was doing sipping hot tea in a newsroom toilet.

Stan had a summer home in New Hampshire. He loved to show it off because it was right on a lake with its own boat and dock. There's no point having a handsome house if nobody knows you have it, so the place was always full with guests. He wanted me to act as his hostess. He suggested I leave things there. I used to do that when I had a house in the Hamptons. It always meant having the outfit I wanted to wear in the country while the belt to it with the matching shoes lay forgotten in my city place. I don't do country well. It's not my thing.

His acreage featured a mossy pond with lily pads floating on the top. I kept careful watch lest Juicy end up in it. "Please," said Stan. "Nobody and nothing has fallen into that pond in the seven years I've had the place. She'll be fine."

The servants' quarters just through the trees did bacon and eggs every other Sunday. Finding her way to that screen door the first weekend in residence, Juicy was rewarded with tiny bits of bacon. This particular Sunday, when the succulent aroma was so strong wafting out of that kitchen in New Hampshire that it clung to the hillsides as far away as Vermont, she raced in that direction. So intent was she that *boom*! down into that green sludge stocked with fish went the Juice. The pond was sufficiently large that there was no way to stand along the rim and collect her. And I didn't exactly have a long-handled colander on me.

I had to wade in and splash around and reach around as Juicy sputtered. Wet and scared and shivering and looking like a green rat, I held her out in my two hands and went chasing for a towel.

The next day the planned entertainment was showing off the boat. "Take the dog," Stan said. "It'll be fun."

"This dog's never been on a boat."

"She'll love it," he said.

"But she's never been on a boat," I said.

"She'll love it," he said.

"Look, this beauty won't go in the shower with me. Won't go out if it rains. At the beach she shies from the shoreline. She tolerates but doesn't really love baths. And I think she already had her aquatic experience yesterday."

"All dogs love swimming."

"Mine doesn't like water."

"She'll love it," he said. "My friends Edith and Henry's dogs love it."

"Who are Edith and Henry?"

"My friends."

"What kind of dogs do Edith and Henry have?"

"Labs."

"*Labs?*"

"Labradors."

"I *know* what Labs are. They eat more than this one weighs."

"She'll love it."

His motorboat, *The Ebit,* was a gift from a grateful CEO whose creative arithmetic could have nailed him if not for Stansfield's ability in front of a jury. *Ebit* stood for examination before interest and taxes. As each wave crested, my dog became more agitated. She wouldn't sit or lie down or stay still. We cut across a cigarette boat's wake. *The Ebit* pitched and rolled, and Juicy slid back and forth, squeaking and yelping. *The Ebit* rode high in the water. As it rocked back down, Stan threw the engine into drive. It bobbed, then surged ahead with a chug, and he yelled at me, "Hold on to the dog," just as Juicy took a header right off the port side. Or would have had I not grabbed her back chicken legs.

I liked Stan. I didn't love him. I liked him.

In the end, I didn't think we should continue in lockstep. Me, stepmother to three cats? I don't think so. And being automatically paired as a couple with Stan, I missed the best friends in the world. Those who were A-number-one in their professions or the tops—at least in my mind—in terms of humor or joie de vivre or enjoying life or whatever. Hard to tie up the world's talents and smarts and accomplishments all in one person. We use different emotional and intellectual muscles with different people. In fact, we *are* different people with different people.

I realized I was very happy the way I was. I'd plowed through bad years and was now quite content with my life.

Only in testing out new people and new ways can you find what fits for you. I had wonderful friends. I treasured my friends. I just wasn't up for devoting myself to any two-legged creature.

I thought to myself, Jazzy, honey, you spoiled it for me. You and your relatives are the only species I want in my arms. And then I thought: The facts were plain. I was going to the dogs.

SIX

It's Okay to Fall in Love Again

 I'd say Juicy was becoming obstreperous, but the word is bigger than the dog.

Juicy was acting out. My knee-jerk nervous-mother reaction was to try to placate her. Not train her—professional trainers begged me never to mention I'd ever been their client—just placate her. I always felt unhappy leaving this creature by herself. Whenever I was anywhere and I knew she was alone, I felt pushed to rush home and take care of the Yorkshire terrier who owned me.

The night presidential candidate John Kerry had a political fund-raiser, it was Whoopi Goldberg, the Dave Matthews Band, Paul Newman, Bon Jovi, a cast of thousands. The evening started with a cocktail party, then a long show at Radio City Music Hall, followed by the VIPs heading to a private dinner. It was a late night.

This was the typical kind of gala where I'd just nonstop

work. During the cocktail portion, I'd catch the stars. There's no way to juggle a glass, a plate, a fork, a napkin, and a pad and pencil, so I'd run around getting quotes while they all vacuumed up the pâté and caviar. Later, at the official sit-down dinner time, when the shrimp and steak and lobster and salmon en croûte and veal en gelée and mile-high desserts are being served, I'd be phoning it in. I never get food. It's what I call my typical I-always-end-up-eating-tuna-at-home evening.

Believe me, I'm at an age where I'm allowed to stay out late. I mean, I'm even permitted to cross the streets by myself. But this night I needed to get home. The problem was, Juicy was alone. I needed to get home. My escort, a friend who's a political insider, wasn't planning to move that quickly. He needed to shake hands. He also needed to shake something else. He whispered in my ear that he had to get to the john before he got to the car.

I wanted out of there. I was in a hurry. Juicy's not exactly a barnyard latchkey cur. The picture of that tiny feather just sitting there waiting for me made me anxious. I'd heard of another tiny dog who, when repeatedly left alone, had withered away to a point almost of death. Juicy was all I could think about. Besides, I'd already weaseled out whatever information I needed from the evening, so I quick scrambled into my friend's car.

He was an old friend, but I suddenly became aware that some parts of him had gotten a little too old. The car started up. So did he. "Listen, I have to go," he said.

"Hold it in."

"Can't."

"Oh, please," I said. "It'll take two minutes to drop me off. I'm only a few blocks from here."

"I know, but I have to pee."

"You're forty-eight years old. You peed enough."

"I have to pee."

"Where? It's after midnight. No restaurants are open around here. Where do you want to go?"

The car pulled to the curb. There was a subway kiosk on the corner. In the shadows, nearly invisible on the ground, sat a bum sipping from a container of coffee. My friend didn't see this homeless guy. He started to do what comes naturally when the bum rumbled: "Pal, you're peeing in my dining room."

Startled, my friend hustled back and folded himself into the safety of the Caddy's interior. A block farther and this guy could contain himself no longer. We pulled over again. It was elegant Park Avenue. Manicured trees and white-gloved doormen standing guard. My friend opened the car door. Seeing this shiny black limo gliding right to his building, the doorman trundled out to help. My friend, who didn't need help because he knew exactly where it is, whipped it out and aimed it at a tree.

With the doorman still standing there, he clambered back in and said to me, "So what do you tip for a thing like that?"

———

The lunacy of my experiences thanks to what was now a three-pounder upstairs was compounding. She'd developed the annoying habit of barking maniacally when the house phone rang. Not the regular telephone. Just the intercom on the kitchen wall, which as she'd fast determined, meant someone was coming up. Early on she equated that special ring with the imminent arrival of another human being for her to sniff. At its sound Cindy's dog became Pavlov's dog. You'd think this creature was a Bernese mountain dog the way she began barking. You could've heard her in Rangoon. And never did she stop. She had lungs bigger than her whole body. The house phone became useless because we could never hear what the doorman was saying.

There was the afternoon I was at QVC's Pennsylvania headquarters. Heavy traffic delayed my drive home, and I was due at a sit-down for Walter Cronkite at seven. I hadn't seen my baby all day; however, I couldn't spare even two seconds because I had exactly fifteen minutes to change and dress. I called Nazalene to put the TV on high and unlatch the front door so, if I took off my shoes, I could slip in without Juicy hearing me. Once she heard me, I'd have to shower her with attention. Here I was tiptoeing into my own home and tiptoeing out. Sneaking out on my dog! It was ludicrous.

My born-again bitch did not like being untended or unnoticed. There was that Tuesday I was out of the house with back-to-back appointments. Due in, while I was away, was an out-of-town houseguest who was going with me to a dressy dinner party. Unexpectedly, my houseguest had run into her friend Val Kilmer, and somehow, en route, Val had decided to join us. My houseguest was changing clothes at my apartment. Movie star Val's wardrobe consisted of what he was wearing—grungy flip-flops, torn jeans, and a tee. And although I never quite got the dynamics correct, his luggage for some reason was in Santa Fe, where he lives.

He went out to Barneys, a nearby department store. The salespeople, recognizing Val Kilmer, ran around for him. He spent thousands on a suit, shirt, cuff links, tie, shoes, and socks. Dinner was at eight. By seven he was back in my living room.

Nazalene was trying to ready my things for the evening, pressing a strange houseguest's blouse, and with no advance notice, suddenly racing around for Val Kilmer. She was temporarily not able to pay full mind to the bitch in residence. Juicy resented such busyness. Everyone rushing about. Val needed shaving cream. Juicy had other issues. She had a totally different agenda. She didn't need shaving cream. She needed attention.

Juicy crowned this Mack Sennett comedy by pooping on the living room rug, which if we hadn't had a houseguest wouldn't have been accessible to her in the first place because we'd have had our doggy gate up. As my home was turning into an animal shelter, I called from the outside, only to learn that Val Kilmer was looking for a room to shower in and change.

Juicy couldn't ask for a man-to-man sit-down to discuss her problems. She couldn't book an additional forty-five-minute session with her shrink. So in place of the usual "Good girl, good girl" praise, she was garnering more attention of the "bad girl, bad girl" variety. She was doing bad doggy things.

I took her to a screening. The movie turned out to be lousy. And my Yorkie turned out to be a critic. About twenty minutes in she grew unhappy. She flounced about in my arms, which were somewhat filled since they were also balancing an economy-size bucket of popcorn. Then, without warning, Juicy darted into the empty lap next to me. It belonged to an advertising exec I know. However, I did not need to know him as well as I suddenly got to know him. Mr. Advertising Exec had obviously come from a big dinner. To allow himself maximum breathing room, he had unzipped his fly. When this furry creature with the floor-length Fu Manchu mustache and the extended tiny pink tongue unexpectedly careened onto him, he hastily made to zip up. It was too hastily. Her long hair got caught in his zipper . . .

Don't ask.

There was the lunchtime we visited business associates in a nearby hotel. A food tray had been left in front of a suite across the hall. The lovers inside finally opened their door a crack, and Juicy, who'd been nosing around their chopped sirloin, rappelled onto their bed.

For me, nothing was too much for her. I hired a massage therapist who fingered her bones, ribs, tickled her under the chin, and kneaded his fingers into her stomach and onto her head for an hour. It cost me seventy-five dollars to have him do what I usually did every day for free.

And anytime I went away she went off. The instant I'd start packing, Juicy would stand rigid in the doorway, never taking her eyes off me. Such a smart animal. She knew to align those big clunky things getting hauled out of the luggage closet with my leaving her. She positioned herself against the doorjamb. Not even for the thrill of jumping on a squirrel would she let me alone. While I was folding and fluffing and stuffing, I took off the familiar black boxy jacket, one with patch pockets that I wear for traveling, and placed it on a chair. It dropped on the floor. This dog planted her teeny butt right on the lapel so the jacket and I couldn't go without her.

She accompanied me to the airport, and I took her with me into the ladies' room. Inside the stall my heart suddenly stopped. Having doubled the loop on the leash around a hook inside my stall, I knew she was safe—but she'd disappeared. My dog was gone. The leash was played out to its fullest leading to my left, but where the hell was Juicy! I was in a busy ladies' room in a frenetic airport inside a cubicle, and Juicy wasn't with me. I panicked. Scrooching down, I peered under the cubicle and saw, to my left, a pair of high heels. Okay, fine. Nice shoes, by the way. Jimmy Choo. And then I saw the purse of the owner of the shoes. It was on the floor near her feet. The purse was not closed. And in it was an open cellophane bag of pretzels. And who was sitting happily inside this lady's handbag eating her pretzels?

Juicy!

Oh, God. Understand, this is not exactly the kind of social situation that calls for introductions. What am I going to do, say hello to the Jimmy Choo shoes, introduce myself charmingly with "Hi there, I write a column for the *New York Post,* and, please, I'm not some kind of sick sex pervert, but if you don't mind, it seems my dog Juicy is in your toilet licking your pretzels"?

I tugged, but Juicy was burrowed inside the purse and the leash wouldn't lift her out. I whispered. In a subdued but anguished voice I called her name. Finally, a pair of eyes leaned down almost at the level of the Jimmy Choos and, wide and slightly in terror, met mine, whereupon I explained to the Eyes the best I could and dragged my snacking dog out of her handbag and toward the front door.

I got in the habit of trying to take Juicy everywhere, even places she didn't belong, because I figured she was lonely.

A couple of colleagues have a home right on a golf course next to a dowager who looked like Elizabeth of England's grandma, the long gone dowager Queen Mary. White coiffed hair, ramrod straight spine, hand-carved cane, bejeweled choker, generally dour mien. On a particularly early morning walk, this dowager told me I mustn't spoil my dog. And then she turned and smiled earring to earring when her own pet, a papillon, went potty. "Aha!" she exclaimed. "Well formed. Good boy, Sloan."

Their manicured lawn, which looked like emerald green velvet, was actually the ninth hole. My dog was running around happily. Juicy, unfortunately, does not know the protocol of the game of golf. To her a ball is something you pick up, put in your mouth, slobber all over, run with, and drop elsewhere. Which she did. Some geezer who had a thousand-dollar bet on that particular putt nearly had Juicy Adams euthanized.

We played catch together. We bathed together, walked together, partied together. At one cocktail do a doctor put wine on his pinkie, and my dog, clearly an incipient lush, licked it off. You can't take friends for granted. You have to give them attention lest they drift away. Although dogs are always categorized as giving "unconditional love," forget it. It's conditional. I'd read a book that said you should have talks with your pet. So, we chatted. I even snuck Juicy into a no-dogs-allowed event by shoving her in a bag and arranging for pals already inside to climb through a break in a fence and lift the bag from me. I then, dogless, sashayed through the security and reclaimed my unconditional love.

A psychiatrist invited us for a playdate. The lady had a cat. The cat freaked Juicy so much that she dove under the bed and stayed there cowering. A wuss in front of a puss. This was the animal who was supposed to protect me? Clearly I was never to see a sign outside my home reading: BEWARE OF YORKIE.

When the terrace door was open, Juicy would throw herself over the threshold but wouldn't cross it. No pawing. No scratching. Just lie there until I, personally, came to accompany her outside, whereupon she'd bark happily at sundrenched bushes the odd moments they danced in the breeze. We enjoyed lots of lazy time together. A spoon of iced tea with Sweet'n Low in the afternoon and then I'd inquire of her if it tasted all right.

On a week in the country a groundsman drove us in his noisy jouncy pickup. Juicy scratched around and circled around and crawled up my arm and whined and generally was visibly loudly cranky. Eventually she shut up and settled down when we discovered a knitted afghan bunched under her did the trick. The whole five days I dragged about clutching an old seedy multicolored not particularly clean afghan. Finally, we stuck her in a purring Jaguar. She was comfy.

I recognized it was my nontraining that had produced such a spoiled little girl, but there it was, that was what I had. I took her to a playdate with a Westie in the Hamptons. She ended up with a bite from a red ant. She extended her paw to me. She was yelping. She was like a baby with a boo-boo, and when the Westie's owner laughed, the yelping stopped dead. Juicy, with her big round eyes, gave the owner a glare like "Who the hell do you think you are to laugh at me? I am injured." Being a neurotic mother, I fussed over her. I kissed the boo-boo. She then reextended her paw and yelped again.

Juicy didn't know she was a dog. This Hampton house was overly drafty, so I'd preheat a towel, then fold it into the bottom of her bed. Sometimes I'd put a lightly filled hot water bottle in it inside a pillowcase. Every morning she'd get snuggled and massaged and rubbed and kissed. She waited for it. Even the morning she had a tummy upset she wouldn't wiggle off until after her ten minutes of cuddling. That morning she first whoopsed, then went kissy-kissy. Trust me, this takes only a mother's love. And Pepto-Bismol.

The housekeeper made an apricot pie. The fragrance of this homemade deliciousness wafted through the whole house. We knew not to sample it, because it was for a party that night. The housekeeper set it down on a low stool to cool. It cooled all right. Mostly inside Juicy's stomach. The dinner party then got topped with a store-bought box of Mallomars.

Juicy even did a showbiz interview. Bruiser, the Chihuahua who costarred with Reese Witherspoon in those *Legally Blonde* things, selected fellow VID Juicy as his personal reporter. The movie's writer arranged it. Bruiser told her: "I'm already six. Although I don't look my age, I make an effort to watch calories. My mother's the Taco Bell dog. We stars know there's always young hound dogs coming up. You have to watch your figure."

Juicy inquired what he weighed. Barked Bruiser: "I don't give out that information. Let's just say I'm around five pounds."

I personally heard Juicy bark something like "Oooh, you

sly dog." As they woofed good-bye, Bruiser expressed a desire to come to New York with "And my dream is to pee on the Observation Floor of the Empire State Building."

Juicy was a pro. It was a nifty interview.

In the moonlight I looked at the little bristle that stuck out around the tips of her ears and sideburns. In the sunlight I looked at the millimeter of silvery beige hairs that fluttered off her teeny tail. In the daylight I kissed her ears, which were the shape of asparagus tips. And all the ladies who saw her kissed her. And she let them. And she'd preen. A born diva.

It kept on that, in the middle of high-profile evenings— ones people would sell their firstborn to get invited to—I'd run home like a scared rabbit. Upon arriving there, I'd plop to the floor and, in the safety of my kitchen, play with my gorgeous-faced terrier. I'd throw a squeaky toy. She, who seemed to have graduated beyond this mindless activity, would look at me like "Oh, for God's sake, you going to do that dumb thing again?" and wouldn't even run after it. I'd end up throwing it and running after it and coming back with it and throwing it again and retrieving it again. The dog was lying flat out, I was racing around.

Juicy was so smart. When she wanted affection, she'd teeter on her hind legs, scratch at me in a begging motion with both paws until I'd scrooch down to her, nose to nose, and we'd both go kissy-kissy. I came back from some quickie drop-in at some party wearing a new red and black Joanna Mastroianni suit with a self-hankie tacked into the pocket.

In her kissing mode, this ballet dancer was en pointe doing the begging motion with both paws. But she conned me. I bent down for the anticipated kiss. Ignoring my face, she grabbed the handkerchief out of my pocket.

Juicy was deliberately trying my patience because she knew when it came to me she could get away with anything. I actually had a fight with her. She'd become fascinated by a full-length mirror. She discovered that if she perched at a specific spot at the far edge of the bed, she could see herself. She would then bark endlessly at this animal gazing straight back at her. If I covered the glass, she'd bark because she could no longer see what she knew was there. If I uncovered it, she'd bark because, again, she was staring at this mirror image. If I tried to show her it was just her own reflection, she'd bark at whatever was unfolding in her doggy head that I couldn't understand. Whatever, she was obsessed and I was distressed.

I hollered at this tiny terrier like she was a real person. I turned my back on her. I refused to talk to her. Suddenly, the insanity of my behavior washed over me. I thought, My God, I'm losing it. I'm actually considering this dog my human equal. It's like I'm telling off my real birth child, "If you continue acting like this I'll have nothing to do with you anymore."

Robert Lahita, the autoimmune diseases specialist who's listed in every compendium of New York's top doctors, and his wife, Terry, and I always precede our dinners with a two-hour visit to some museum. While Juicy was into this Operation Mirror period, the Lahitas and I had gone to the Natural History Museum, which was holding a DNA exhibition. Mine was tested. Juicy's was tested. The Lahitas' were tested. The strains of other dogs were tested. Juicy's DNA and my DNA measured out to be less than five percentage points away from one another.

What that meant to a scientist, I don't know. What it meant to me, I knew. It meant, "Juicy, hon, you and me, we're closer than biological mommy and child. We're practically one."

It was only, basically, when I was right with her that Juicy was a happy camper. As twilight descended one gentle evening, we were locked in each other's arms. I whispered to her, "Juicy, baby, someday we'll sit on a porch in a rocking chair and stroke our bottles of pills together." She licked my face. I picked her up with one hand and, nose to nose, said, "If the time comes we can't even kiss anymore, worse comes to worse we can always gum one another."

That night my lawyer friend Arlene came over. Pet lover Arlene has three cats. She hugged and cuddled my Juicy. She snuggled her and nuzzled her. Then the doorbell rang. Other friends were arriving. Hurrying to join the rest of the team, Arlene, from her five-nine height, just dropped Juicy. To her it was a reflex action. In Arlene's head, Juicy was a cat. And that's what you do with cats. Drop them. And they always end up right side up.

Juicy's a dog. Arlene dropped her. She stayed there. The

kitchen floor is stone. This tiny dog's bones are the size of filaments. She did not get up.

My heart stopped. The only creature I had left to call my own and whom I loved desperately had just gotten hurt.

Arlene looked at me in anguish. Juicy lay there. Arlene, who was now in worse shape than Juicy, was distraught. And I was in worse shape than either of them. Crying, fumbling, panicking, the two of us bundled her into a blanket. The vet was busy handling another calamity but ran out to attend Juicy. No broken bones. Just a strain or sprain. We were told to keep her off that one hurt leg. To watch her carefully.

God, was she watched carefully. The whole household stayed up all night. For four nights. We all watched her carefully. Bit by bit she could twitch. Then she limped. Then she wobbled. Then she walked. Then she ran.

Only then did I breathe.

But my devoted daughter had become catatonic. This once noisy yapper was now hiding. Call her name, she wouldn't come. Search for her, she wouldn't be found. Juicy was going under. She was burrowing into dark corners. Under a chair. Into a remote corner. Behind some discarded box. Curling fetus-style into dark and distant places. Pick her up, she offered no resistance. Stroke her, she was unresponsive.

Paula, who had brought both Jazzy and Juicy into the world, called. "I don't know," I said. "Juicy's not right."

"Does she sleep with you as usual?"

"Well, she's on the bed with me as usual, but she's stand-offish. She won't cuddle."

"Look, when she came to you she had a brother. Today she's an only child. Alone. It's as though she's blaming you for things."

I didn't know what to say to that, so I said nothing. Paula then asked, "Does she sleep?"

"No."

"How do you know?"

"Because I don't either."

"She restless?"

"No."

"What's she doing?"

"Nothing. Lying there with her eyes open."

"You have to get her out of this condition."

"I have to first get myself out of this condition."

"Look, you won't like hearing what I'm going to say, but the fact is you have to get another dog."

"Please. This is stupid. It is not my idea to get my heart broken yet again. I can barely breathe I am so distressed. I. Am. Not. Getting. Another. Dog," I snapped.

Between breeding, boarding, grooming, owning, and showing, Barnhill Kennels in Woodbury, Connecticut, maintains a hundred dogs a day. This quintessential dog lover then said: "Right now it isn't even about you. It's about Juicy."

"Get off it."

"I'm telling you, you have to get another dog."

"And I'm telling you, not a chance. I cannot go through this again."

The next morning I was still in my galabia, the white cotton floor-length Arab shirt that's standard men's dress in the Middle East and is what I sleep in. I had a visitor. Paula had driven down from Connecticut and presented herself in my lobby.

"I brought you a dog," she said quietly.

I shouted at her. "Are you some sort of crazy person who's determined to kill me? Get away from me. Are you thinking that I need some other four-legged creature to pad around my house? I do not want another animal. I do not want some other nice plain lovely generic pet. I do not desire just some dog dog.

"Don't you understand? Don't you speak English? What is the matter with you? The only other dog I want is my Jazzy. Can you give me back Jazzy? Jazzy is the only dog I want. Jazzy!"

From somewhere surrounding her ample person, Paula produced two squiggling bodies. How she made them appear, I don't know. But once on what to them was unfamiliar ground, they went into sniffing, exploring, and barking mode.

Juicy raised her head. These two infidels were invading her terrain. Her eyes locked on them. Scurrying around like rats, they pounced onto what had been her favorite chew toy. A red-and-white crocheted ball with layers of lumps and bumps. Threads hung from it. Since a favorite game was her glomming onto it, followed by my trying to wrench it from her clenched teeth, she'd practically shredded the thing. But ratty or tatty, it was *hers*. She loved it. And who were these interlopers tossing around her personal belongings!

"Look," I whispered. "Her tail is up."

We watched. The two infidels padded closer. They circled. One darted smack into her space. Juicy grrrred, and the emboldened one scampered away. Juicy stood rigid. This same bold one came close in again to sniff. Juicy snapped at its face. I became fearful Juicy would hurt them. After all, she was older. Not bigger. Just older. They were four months old. She was thirteen months.

Paula re-collected Juicy. This time not to perk her up but to calm her down. Whereas before we couldn't get her to start, now we couldn't get her to stop. She vaulted from Paula's lap and tore after the two. This born-again Dragon Lady nipped one's ear. We heard the squeal. The one nipped wasn't giving up, however. Back it went to tangle or tumble or whatever it took to make the hostess's acquaintance. Like Nazimova, Juicy swanned into the newcomer again.

We separated them. I picked up mine. Paula scooped up hers. "My two are also girls," she said. "And the truth is girls are pushy. These were from the day they were born."

I eyed the sisters, who as yet had no names. I didn't cotton to them. They were descended from the same line as Jazzy. They had his face. The features were so similar that you could see him in them. The likeness made me nervous. Their overfriskiness also made me nervous. They weren't delicious, they were annoying.

"You've got to admit," said Paula, watching the sparring carefully, "that at least Juicy has waked up. She sure has come back out into the light."

We set the trio down again, and once more they began fighting and snarling. The arrivals jumped on Juicy to sniff her. She ran, turned, and started barking. "It isn't that she's come alive because she likes them," I said. "It's that she doesn't like them. They're upsetting her. They're irritating her. I don't want her unhappy. I want her happy."

"Look, I know how you feel and I understand you're not ready, but the fact remains you have to think about another dog," Paula said. "Like these girls or not, in five minutes they brought Juicy back to life."

I stared at the new arrivals some more. "These girls are not for me," I said. "They're too competitive. Way too aggressive. I don't even like how they look. I do not want them to own Jazzy's face. I do not want to gaze at a second-class Jazzy lite.

"Listen, I really do not want another dog. And I guess if I did, which I don't, but if I did because I needed that to save Juicy, I would want another boy. Juicy was accustomed to a brother. Besides, these two girls are much bigger than Juicy, even though they're younger. I don't want any newcomer bossing Juicy around."

Paula unzipped a floppy tote bag she'd had crumpled under her arm. From its depths, one hand plucked out a squiggly, squirmy three-month-old. A boy. Tiny. One pound, fourteen ounces. His stubby coat resembled fake fur.

Whereas gorgeous Juicy had a long body, silky silvery hair, and almost ankle-length Fu Manchu golden whiskers, this Yorkie was square. Chunky and chubby. His pitch-black fur was stubby. And he stood where Paula had placed him.

"This one's a wuss," she said.

"He doesn't look like anybody in the family," I said. "He has fat cheeks. He's like a real life Gund or Steiff teddy bear. He's absolutely one of those stuffed animals in a toy store."

"He shares the family ancestry. Same father as Juicy, same mother as Jazzy. It was only two in the litter. He has a twin. The brother is smaller. One pound, eleven ounces. The reason I didn't bring the twin is he's having a low-blood-sugar problem. I'm watching him carefully. Feeding him honey off my finger. One thing I know you don't need is a dog who's sick."

This little one propelled himself forward maybe an inch. The movements were herky-jerky. He hopped around like a battery-operated windup toy.

This time Juicy was the aggressor. She trotted over and smelled him. He stood there. Then he hopped back to Paula's protective custody. Juicy followed. It was a ballet. Lying flat on the floor, I picked up this tiny round fur muff. And he licked me. And I was gone.

I draped him around my throat and held him in position with one hand. My chin and my fingers cuddled him. He stayed. Didn't fight. Juicy never took her eyes away. She wanted him back down. She wanted to examine him, and she wanted me not to hold him or love him. Looking up at him hanging on my neck, she barked. I set him down gingerly. When the girls started harassing him, Paula grabbed them. I took turns cuddling and hugging Juicy and this boy baby as they investigated each other. I threw a toy. She commandeered it. He let her. I threw a chew stick. Each grabbed an end. He let her get it.

"He's a wuss," repeated Paula.

A new carpet had been laid in the small areaway from my apartment to the elevator. It had taken years for the building's board to vote for the redecoration plan. It had taken months for the final choice in décor to be made. That very morning the rug had been laid. The moment the carpenters hammered the last tack and said bye-bye, this brand-new little being inaugurated this brand-new beige-and-black carpet, which instantly osmosed into beige and darker beige and black.

I went to work. On my knees. Scrubbing the spot. A touch of vinegar. Baby wipes. Stuff that removes odors from fabric. Later, when nobody in that hallway was stirring, with a hairpin I painstakingly plumped back up each fiber of the weave. After my great cleaning job, the hairs had ended up lying sideways, and I couldn't risk those tufts looking mangled or swabbed, because early that evening the redecorating committee was scheduled to come to inspect.

Midway in this expanse of standing up hairs was that small bald slightly darker spot. When the committee arrived, one pair of eyes noted that there appeared to be—although she was certain she was mistaken because this carpet was brand-new—a verrrry slight discoloration in one place. She inquired of the decorator if the carpet might be faulty and should they so inform the manufacturer? I hastily sputtered, "No, no no. I don't know what you're talking about. Must be the lighting. To my eyes it looks perfect."

This precious being fascinated me. He trembled. He shrunk back into himself, becoming even smaller if that were possible. I stuck him down my shirt. His little head peeked out. It was the size of a plum. I rumpled the top of his head. He chewed at the button of my galabia. And then he licked my neck. It was clear. This one already owned me.

"I have three more I'll bring tomorrow for you to see," said Paula.

"No," I said. "Never mind. Forget it. I'm stuck on Jazzy Junior."

"Jazzy Junior?"

"Jazzy Junior."

"J.J.?"

"Jazzy Junior."

I announced to Paula I was taking Jazzy Junior.

"We playing Yorkie Roulette again? Jazzy Junior going to be shuttled back and forth like Juicy was?"

Something warm was licking my bare foot. I told Paula: "Juicy and I are accepting Jazzy Junior right now as a full-fledged member of the Adams family."

I looked down in time to see Juicy barrel smack into the side of her new brother. I then saw her ruffle and snuggle him. I thought, Jazzy Adams Junior, welcome to the hood.

Juicy was happy. I was happy. We were all in love again.

SEVEN

A Good Marriage Is About Compromise

Starting all over with a puppy again? Again with the eating new shoes and biting old tables? I was too weary to start with a third puppy in as many years. It's why grandparents can't rear grandkids. Go find the energy to start training yet another baby.

Once more it was teaching the potty prompt. At 6:00 A.M., my wake-up time, I would hit the powder room and right away plop Jazzy Junior on his spread-out paper. Nothing. My bladder being way older, the only one of us who had to go was me. I would repeat the process two hours later. We both were in position in that same room again at eight. Me, I went. Him, he didn't. I got the feeling he was thinking, Why's this dumb lady sticking me in this corner every minute? I'll pore over this newspaper when I'm ready. Frustrated with those obedience tricks the books provided, I'd finally pluck him up and we'd both leave the john. He would then lurch direct to the doggy stairs I had specially made for him to reach my bed and let it all out there. Another time, when his needs were different, he negotiated a faux leopard doggy ramp which was parked at my work space. He left his present smack on my desk.

Our new nuisance kept Juicy on the go. He was so annoying that it forced Juicy out of her funk.

Jazzy Junior was in residence maybe a hot five days when I had to get myself together to do a TV show. Lisa my hairdresser came over. Whether it was the chemicals or the hair spray, Juicy, who was not very close to other females, had never cottoned to Lisa.

Two weeks earlier Lisa had come over to do a quick comb-out. She'd made the mistake of throwing her bag and coat and parcels across a table that was above Juicy's favorite guest room bed. *Her* personal bed. The heart-shaped faux sable bed that bore *her* blanket. That had *her* aroma. Juicy had gotten upset. She backed away and stared at Lisa. This guest room, which is off the kitchen, which is basically the family room, has a sofa and a rocking chair. Juicy, choosing not to leap onto any other perfectly good place, choosing not to pad into the kitchen, where all of us were, just stood there. Staring. Lisa eventually had to move her belongings. Following every remnant of Lisa being removed from *her* area, Juicy jumped into her regular spot and, after commanding it for some moments, sauntered into the kitchen while ignoring Lisa.

It was now two weeks later, and circumstances were different. Jazzy Junior was in residence. Juicy was into reassessing her options. She'd always had an attitude. Now she had it louder. Lisa arrived, and Juicy went into overdrive. Leapt into her arms. Barked happily. Licked her. Demanded her attention. Lisa mindfully threw her coat down in another spot. Juicy forsook her usual throne, pounced smack in the center of Lisa's coat, and rolled around in it.

"What's with Juicy?" Lisa asked. "She usually couldn't care less about me. What happened?"

Junior was what happened.

My two baby Yorkies shared the same ancestry and were born in the same time frame a year apart—Juicy on July 29, Junior on May 31, but they had different personalities. In terms of sleeping, Juicy curls snaillike right into my side or under my arm. Junior toddles to the top of the pillow and burrows into the middle of my teased hair. Pre-Junior, I could coax a second day out of a beauty salon visit. Now, forget it. He makes a nest out of my head.

At four months and maybe three days, this nesting was not so adorable. I remember an early fall morning. It was dark. Junior is also dark. I'd hoisted myself out of bed, taken one giant step, and all 120 pounds of me crashed onto Junior. In trying to avoid stepping on him, I'd done a tour jeté on the polished wood floor and gashed my forehead. Later, when I laid this traumatized head on the pillow and my newest child jumped—all four paws—onto it . . . Don't ask.

The truth is, a husband will get mad at you, a relative will criticize you—but even when you're thoughtless, your animals will only love you. When I smashed down around him, Junior's yelp could've been heard round the world. Two days later he forgave me. I have a second cousin who still remembers that when he was twelve and sick his mother left him alone although she took off from work when their shih tzu was not well. The cousin is now thirty-six. He still throws it up to his mother.

Jazzy Junior also performs rituals. Prior to bedding down he walks around. What he walks around and on is me. My face and my body. He trots up and down my stomach. And mine is no washboard stomach. Mine is more like a water bed. I don't care what dietitians tell you, I still eat late. Therefore, the stomach this dog is running on top of is full. And he trampolines right onto it either from the top doggy stair or straight off the bones of playmate Juicy. Granted, he weighs less than say for instance, Schwarzenegger, but if in the middle of the darkness a live dog suddenly vaults onto the center of your gut, it's not terrific. And if I put on the light for whatever reason, he puts his paws over his eyes.

He also patrols my chest. He claws as though to clear away the leaves and underbrush and make himself comfy. Now, I don't have a whole load of leaves and underbrush on my chest. Also, I don't know the standard thickness of most nighties, but mine are not the equivalent of chain mail, and this scratching with his footnails hurts. He then pads around and around in a circle until whatever it is that he needs to satisfy him has satisfied him. The next move is to collapse full length. Always with the tail and tushy pointing straight up my nose. Only after a five-minute rest does he pick himself up and settle down inside my hair. I asked an animal behaviorist why he does these things, and she answered: "How do I know? What am I, a Yorkie?"

My babies had captured my heart, but bit by bit they were taking the rest of me, too. Junior was into snoring. Whatever larynx, esophagus, or any other canal he has in him has to be so small it would almost seem to make no difference. So how he has a loud snore, I don't know. But one night I was sleeping on the superfinest pure silk. Decorator Carleton Varney had been to an auction and snapped up a set of hand-embroidered rose-colored silk sheets. From some sale of Imelda Marcos's household goods, they were embroidered with "Imee," the name of Imelda's daughter. Carleton gave them to me, and we'd dressed the bed with them that night.

Junior was pawing the area he was readying for his lie-down. It happened to be two days before Ana the groomer came for the monthly manicuring, and Junior's nails had reached a length somewhere between the Dowager Empress of China's and Barbra Streisand's. This particular time what he was clawing, scratching, and destroying, just like he was some cruddy outdoor junkyard mutt, was the historic silk sheet stretched across my rumpled belly. My bed has no pebbles to unloose or earth to hoe. Still he circled, then pawed, then scratched, and his nails dug through clear down to my blood vessels. He methodically shredded my lone, one-and-only, rose-colored, hand-embroidered former First Lady of the Philippines top silk sheet.

On this particular eight-hour stretch, everything was working for Junior and against me. He finally fell asleep, but his snoring kept me up. I tried lying on one side to bury my best hearing ear in the pillow. I stuffed it with Kleenex. I pulled a blanket over my head. Nothing helped.

Because I couldn't sleep I felt hungry. I remembered a muffin on the refrigerator's middle shelf shoved way in the back. I desperately wanted it. I thought about it. I pictured it. I mentally tasted it. The longer I contemplated this the more restless and cranky I became. I tossed and turned. Short of creating an entire disturbance whereby all three of us had to march en masse to the kitchen and back, I could envision no way for that muffin to get down my throat. It was a scene out of Charles Dickens. Like Oliver Twist silently pleading for more porridge, I lay in bed hungry.

I knew if I fed me I'd also have to feed Juicy. Set out food for her and she'd finish before the bowl was placed on the floor. Feed her anytime, she ate. Finish feeding her then feed her again immediately, she ate. Put down food for six visiting dogs, she'd eat hers and then shove them aside to gobble theirs. Give her treats right after her dinner, she ate. Watermelon, ice cream, chicken soup, peaches, broccoli, oatmeal, spareribs, Chinese food, she ate it. She never saw a veal chop she didn't like.

I couldn't understand where she put it. If I got up in the

middle of the night to knock off the lone stiff sardine that had been left moldering on the third shelf in the back of my refrigerator since 1967, I gained four pounds.

Juicy, my darling Juicy, would eat anything. Jazzy Junior was born finicky. Even when he's starving, getting him to eat is a drama. I lie flat on the floor. I hum. I hand-feed. And fie on a spoon. He wants fingers. If not, he walks around. He shows off. Nazalene has a Guyanese expression. "He has to make style," she says.

Junior will only freely eat certain things. I smeared butter pecan ice cream on my finger, and he licked it greedily but picked out the pecans with his paw. If something is not to his liking, he turns his face and pushes it away. When he doesn't want his Eukanubas, he picks them from his bowl and drops them on the floor.

For myself I won't fuss. I'll stand at the fridge and wolf down something that's growing mold on it because it's been there so long. For my kids I'll get out pots, pans, kosher chickens. I'll poach. I'll braise. If I pretend I'm eating something, they'll lap up anything. To encourage Junior, I've sampled dog food. I've chewed dog treats. I've downed doggy everything. Once, to increase his appetite I thought I'd mix in a spoonful of cottage cheese. I first ate a spoonful. The cottage cheese had turned sour. I mixed it with Jell-O and downed it. Later, when I opened a fresh cottage cheese for him, he liked it only with the Jell-O just because that's the way I'd had it.

Worrying he isn't getting sufficient vitamins, I try to

feed him veggies, and he looks at me in doggy disgust. One quiet evening a friend was putting together a dinner that included string beans. While puttering around he was singing. As he held a high operatic note, he looked down, and to his astonishment he saw Jazzy nibbling a forkful of dropped microwaved string beans. He stopped singing to watch. Jazzy stopped eating the string beans. He went back into "La Donna è Mobile," and Jazzy ate more string beans. From then on we would microwave three lousy string beans, do ten minutes of "O Sole Mio," and Jazzy Adams Junior got his veggie vitamins.

It's always a ballet with his food, but Jazzy Junior has almost become a drug for me. I need him. I crave his tiny paws crawling up my body to my face.

So this night, because my innards were gnawing with hunger, I became tense. I developed a headache. Wide awake, I had a laundry list of needs. The first was food. I finally raided the fridge and couldn't find the muffin but did locate some meat loaf from the third shelf in the back, which had probably been there since the year of the Flood. Despite the fact that rigor mortis had already set in to the thing, I quickly inhaled it. I then pounced on something green. We're talking either new cheese or old meat, I have no idea. I didn't care either. I just vacuumed it up. It was 3:00 A.M., and I wasn't trying to be Martha Stewart. By the time I trundled back to bed, both babies were out like lights. Cuddled into the middle of the quilt and each other.

The light of the moon glanced off those little noses that

look like raisins. Juicy's teeny tongue slightly out of her mouth. Jazzy's head rolled onto his front right paw. I couldn't possibly disturb them. So I made do on a couch. A kidney-shaped couch. Don't ask what happened to my sacroiliac. The damage is probably permanent.

In the fall a comforter was rolled at the foot of my bed. Jazzy Junior loved it. He piled into it, bundled himself in the middle of it. It was his playground. The newspapers he'd been trained on must have had too many stories of older lady Demi I-want-Moore and her youthful beau Ashton Kindergarten, because right inside that comforter one midnight there was lots of action. Teeny tiny Junior was trying to Do It to grown-up Juicy. That they're both fixed seemed not to slow them down any more than it does our married politicians.

Fall turned into winter, and I needed that comforter. When I shook it out full length and tucked it around me, Jazzy began whining, then he growled then barked then nipped. It was: How dare you take away my playground? And no matter how I tried shutting him up, he wouldn't. I finally wrapped my own shivering bones in some skinny overly laundered blanket that no longer boasted a nap and gave him back his comforter.

So, do I love him? God, yes. I love him, love him, love him. But would I also say he's a genuine pain in the ass? For sure.

Jazzy Junior's legs are so small and his span so minute

that when he's thirsty he walks right into his water bowl. His paws are inside the dish. I then have to mop up wet paw prints throughout the house.

Whereas Juicy is elegant, Jazzy Junior is scruffy, ragtag, a little beaten-up looking in that his mustache goes in odd directions. And when that teeny face, which were he shaved would be the size of an Immy marble, tilts up at you, it's just as though he's saying, "Love me, love me, love me."

I snuck him into a restaurant in his carry bag, but to be sure he stayed quiet I had to order pasta and salad. I didn't want pasta and salad. I wanted chicken cacciatore. The menu was decided by whichever foods he wouldn't want to fight me for.

This dog has changed all parts of my life, including where I'm invited. He came with me to a party. Jazzy Junior, having earlier had a smidge of diarrhea, scooted the whole length of the lady's beige couch. I have since had made a red satin quilted belly band in which I stuff a sanitary napkin so I can take him visiting to high-class nondog-friendly houses.

After I lost Jazzy, canine specialists told me: Stop worrying about taking out your babies and giving them weekends in the country. They're only a few inches long. They get enough exercise just messing up your closet. They don't need cross-country hikes. Just take them for short walks. So, although I'd had no success with the two together, I still tried hard to learn how to handle the pair on a city stroll.

Ivan the trainer repeatedly gave me lessons. He slapped his own leg lightly, and, off they all went like the Rockettes. Ivan told me:

- Put the same length leash on each.
- Hold the loops in the right hand and, with the left, guide the leashes.
- First position the dogs, then start out with the left foot.
- Use the word "heel" to teach them to stay at that part of your foot.
- Guide them to remain on the left. Something about in the army firearms are on your right side. What that had to do with my doglets, God knows.
- If needed, snap the leash, which jerks them a bit so they obey.

Please. I loved them too much to jerk their heads even a teeny bit. The result was, I couldn't make them do what I wanted, and all three of us knew who was the boss—*them*. But I kept trying. I paraded them up and down inside the apartment, out front of the building, on a quiet side street, in a sleepy park. My coordination unfortunately did not coordinate with theirs. We're not exactly talking a team of Clydesdales going full trot. One sauntered, one sniffed. One spied some sexy looking Scotch terrier across the road and ran *under* him.

Escorting Jazzy and Juicy for their daily airing was becoming a cottage industry. New York's famous novelty store since 1848, Hammacher Schlemmer, came out with a doggy carriage much like a baby pram. I bought it. A cage in front prevented their getting loose. But if they needed release quickly, to open it meant you broke your longest middle nail, lost your patience, needed a sheepskin from MIT to figure how to work the catch, and by then your Fido or Fluffy was doin' what comes natcherly.

I went to Sherpa for matching carry bags. Specially made with multiple pockets for toys, treats, water bottle, poop packets, and compartments for me so I needn't also carry my own purse, which would have meant a third bag. After I'd loaded in their needs plus my own keys, phone, wallet, umbrella, these carriers weighed a ton even without the passengers. Slinging them over both shoulders made me ambulate like the Hunchback of Notre-Dame. Two on one shoulder was impossible. I sloped. I walked on a bias. Carting them by the handles, like two shopping bags, didn't work either. Too heavy. I might as well have been bench-pressing.

Lugging my own gear in my own purse now necessitated schlepping three bags. Porters at the airport have less of a load. And then, what went up the shoulder first? If I wanted something from my personal bag, which was the farthest up my arm, I had to first lower the doggy bag and set it down. If my personal bag was the lowest on my arm and I wanted something from it, when I scrooched my body around to unzip the thing, the doggy bag slid down, slammed into it, and its resident started yelping.

Sherpa's next size carrier, large enough to accommodate both bodies, had more of a structure. Unfortunately, Juicy and Jazzy did not always wish to be tumbled into one another. In the house, in the bed, if they felt like it, fine. In a bag because they have to, *no!* So it was Mike Tyson–Lennox Lewis time, with tossing and tussling atop my shoulder. Then one barked because he wanted out, which left me with the carrying bag on my shoulder plus the wriggling dog in my arms. One wanted out, so the other wanted out, but neither wanted to walk, so it became my personal bag, the carry bag, and two dogs in my arms.

Whenever possible I tried to take them wherever possible. Like my Saturday at the movies. I threw both in their larger carry bag and sat in the rear of the theater, one seat in from the aisle. The little one was restless. Too many smells and noises. When the lights went down I settled him on my lap.

The older one, not to be left behind, began jiggling inside the bag. As I leaned over to cuddle the older one, the little one became unbalanced and jumped off my lap.

Lunging, I grabbed him in an awkward headlock—upside down with his head below my elbow and his tail extending to my nose. I clutched him so tightly to my body he could barely breathe. He started barking, and with my heart beating like a trip-hammer and two thousand eyes turned to blink at me, I ran out on Kevin Costner.

There was the Friday evening I took them to Old Stove Pub, a Long Island steak house which had a porch. They sat quietly on the floor near my feet while I chatted with a friend at the next table, Tom Wolfe. This best-selling writer patted Jazzy Junior, then returned to his sirloin. Jazzy, sensing a kindred spirit plus a delicious meal, jumped onto the empty chair alongside the author of *The Bonfire of the Vanities* and helped himself to Tom's steak.

The three of us would go for walks. Except only two of us would walk; Jazzy, not. Little Juicy would be barreling along. Jazzy, not. Jazzy would sit down. Flat splat on his pratt. Plead, beg, get yourself down on all fours in front of God, man, and whoever is staring at you on the street—and reason with him nose to nose—and . . . nothing. This damn dog was not moving. Fifth Avenue and Fifty-seventh is the center of the universe. Arguably the busiest corner of the globe. It was there at high noon, lunchtime, with everyone rushing about, right smack in a patch of warm sun, that Jazzy decided to prove who was Best in Show. He lay down in the midst of thousands of Nikes, Manolos, and sandals rushing over him and around him.

He bestirred himself only once. Lying full out in front of Tiffany, my coddled treasure perked up when a Brussels griffon, attached to a blonde of a certain age, hopped out of a limo. The blonde paused momentarily to window-shop a display of diamond bangles. Jazzy sprang to attention. All of Jazzy sprang to attention and got seriously busy trying to Do It to this Brussels griffon. The Brussels griffon was also of the male persuasion, but this in no way appeared to arrest Jazzy's assault. I wondered if I had a gay dog.

When the blonde and her companion hustled into Tiffany, Jazzy flopped back into his lethargy. Juicy, raring to go, began nonstop barking. I picked her up lest some three-inch stiletto pierce her, but burdened with parcels, shopping bags, my own tote, plus Juicy's mini carry bag in case she tired, I could not leverage my arms around Jazzy. So, in full view of whoever was viewing this, I tugged at his leash. Had a developer decided to build a building directly on that spot, he'd have had to build the thing *around* Jazzy, because that dog was not moving.

I was perspiring. The packages were slipping, and they were heavy. I was late. And what was unfolding on the street corner was embarrassing. Looking supertall in my hat and spike heels, I was literally pulling this toy dog. A passerby stopped dead in his tracks and shouted at me: "That little dog is not well. He obviously can't walk. What's the matter with you? Do you know what you're doing? That's animal abuse! I'm going to report you!"

Jazzy Junior had grown very accustomed to being adored. I'd taken him for a saunter along Fifty-seventh Street's classiest shops. Being a snob, he's particularly happy around Chanel and seems to raise his leg in the area of Nike. Anyway, as we promenaded, a neighbor came out of Burberry's. She stopped to talk. Jazzy grrrred. We kept chatting. He kept grrrring. "What's the matter with him?" she asked. "I really don't know," I said. "Maybe it's only that you didn't say hello to him."

She blinked at me like I was nuts but obediently reached

for him. He immediately trotted off in the opposite direction. She followed, both arms extended. He wobbled in the other direction. She got down on her knees and coaxed him. Eventually she grabbed him and cootchy-cooed him. A good five minutes later she scrambled back up and we resumed the conversation. Jazzy sat happily and quietly at our feet. Not a single grrrr.

One foggy overcast morning I threw on a pair of junk pants, shapeless T-shirt, and Chinese rubber-soled slippers. No makeup. No hair. Us Adamses went for a long ramble. A half a block away, It happened. My boy beauty saw a bird and tugged in a different direction. The leash tangled around my feet. Down I went.

I was physically unhurt. I was, however, lying like a bundle of wet wash in the gutter when an elegant blonde leading two wolfhounds who were high-stepping in perfect cadence came to a stop at my behind, which was hanging off the curb. Straining to rein in my dog, I shrieked, "Jazzy . . . *Jazzeeeeee!*"

"Ohhh," she trilled. "What an adorable name. Did you take it from that new book the lady just wrote?"

My ego or my pride. Having written a dog book yet now looking like a homeless bum in the street and demonstrating that I had absolutely no control over a breed that wasn't as big as a stuffed teddy bear was not good. I didn't know what to do.

"Uh-uh," I mumbled, shaking my head side to side as she helped me up.

"I read that book about Jazzy the dog." She was now helping to grab up Jazzy the dog. "It was adorable. Did you read it?"

"Uh-huh," I mumbled, bobbing my head up and down.

"So did the dog's name come from the book?"

"No. The book's name came from this dog and his relatives. This is Jazzy Junior of *the* Jazzy family."

She stepped back. Actually, recoiled in horror is what she did. The elegant lady with the perfectly poised prancing wolfhounds looked me up and down. Slowly she asked, "And, so, just exactly who are you?"

Too late, nothing I could do, no place to hide. I bit the bullet. "I wrote that book."

"YOU?"

Pretty flattering, I thought. "Yes, me."

"You wrote *The Gift of Jazzy* book?"

"Yeah."

"I see. Well, I certainly hope you learn how to walk him."

Mortified beyond belief, I finally dragged myself home in time for my telephone interview with cellist Yo-Yo Ma, who had some project he was promoting. I was done in. I was also feeling insecure. I didn't know how to deal with owning two dogs. I couldn't seem to get it together, but I barely had time to think when this world-famous man was on the phone saying: "Despite my odd name, nobody calls me Mr. Ma. Just Yo. All you have to do is think of what Sylvester Stallone would call out to his mother—'Yo, Ma'— and that's me."

Go know such a high-class artiste had such a delicious humor. So, fresh from my disaster, I asked him how one schleps a cello, which is definitely larger and more cumbersome than a teacup Yorkie and her brother.

Said Yo: "The cello weighs ten pounds. I buy a second airplane seat for it. To walk around, I strap it on my back like a knapsack. This way my hands are free, and I can manage to carry at least one other thing."

His cello was big and clunky and didn't mold to his body. My babies were soft and huggable. I figured if Yo could walk about carrying his huge ten-pound cello plus one other thing, I could see my way clear to juggle two piles of fluff that together made about eight pounds.

Back out I went. I put Juicy in her carry bag, slung that over my shoulder, wrenched stubborn Jazzy off the sidewalk, where he was again positioned, picked him up and tucked him tightly under my right arm, and started off. As I paused at the corner stoplight one block away, a woman walking a Rottweiler the size of an SUV asked, "What's wrong with your dog that you're carrying him?" Dog people, though they be perfect strangers, seem to talk to other dog people. I said, "Nothing's wrong. He just wants to be carried." She said, "Then there's something wrong with him."

B.C., Before Canines, I'd considered myself busy. Subsequently I became a maxi multitasker. Used to be I'd just get up in the morning. Now before I even brush my teeth, I take care of *them*. The problem is they don't find my recess period interesting. Playing with them is another of my not strong suits. They are totally disinterested in my bumbling attempts. It was suggested I rent a nature video about wolves because the sounds would get their attention and cause them to interact. I rented it. I alone watched it. They yawned and fell asleep. In *97 Ways to Make a Dog Smile* I read about hiding a treat in one clenched fist and seeing if your dog chooses the correct hand. The book says you must resist the urge to hide nothing in either hand as this your dog will not find amusing. I did the whole nine yards. They found nothing amusing, including me.

There was the morning I was leaving a trail of Eukanuba throughout the house so they could exercise and scamper as they ate and at the same time I was readying to rush out the door with them. Susan Sarandon rang. Susan was in the midst of an upset with my newspaper and was granting them no access as a result. Considering I was possibly the only Postie she was willing to talk with, I was eager to hear she was returning my call.

"My God, between you and your daughter, Eva Amurri, and your guy, Tim Robbins, the family seems to be in every movie there is," I said as impatient Juicy was jumping up and down at my feet.

"Yeah," said Susan. "It's an interesting time for us."

The house phone rang to say the cops were watching Reggie and he couldn't stay double-parked much longer,

Jazzy was scratching my ankles, and I was hastily writing down what Susan was telling me.

"Oh, how interesting," I said, trying to sound as calm and interested as a reporter should while motioning to Nazalene to take the damn dogs down and shove them in the car.

My front door slammed. Not only had Nazalene, Jazzy, and Juicy gone into the car but they'd gone away with it. My ride was history. And I was on the phone saying things such as "Really? . . . Oh, wow!"

These dogs break down all your reserves. They strip away all the pretensions. Juicy and Jazzy Junior are antidotes for those emotional toxins our lives build up. I find myself doing a roster of things for them I would never ever think of doing otherwise. I'm squatting in feathers and silk blotting up pee. I'm picking up poop with pages out of Webster's dictionary because it was all that was grabbable. I'm flat out on a floor letting them prance up and down the length of me. You think I'd ever let a human walk all over me?

Everyone in the business of show business, from those on the periphery to those whose names are above the title, is programmed to show only what he or she wants shown. These creatures make you totally honest. Devoid of all affectation.

After I breakfasted with Chuck Norris, I loved him. The smash 'em, bash 'em, trash 'em, slash 'em, get 'em in the groin martial arts star was a sweetie who drank chocolaty Swiss Miss instead of morning coffee and told me funny stories about getting soused. After one such he added: "My son was driving our car, and I had rolled down the window because, man, was I feeling sick. It was freezing. But ice cold. We were driving along with my head hanging out. Finally my son said, 'Hey, close the window. I'm dying here.' So I closed it, but I put on the air-conditioning."

Such fresh, charming conversation showed an easygoing, un-uptight picture of Chuck. One reader wrote she'd become a fan of his only after reading my column about him. Chuck didn't see it that way. Drinking was not the image he wanted projected. The man was definitely P.O.d at me.

Then there's Alan Alda, who told me: "The biggest misconception about me is that I'm this Goody Two-shoes. I don't know how all this Nice Guy bullshit happened, but that's not really me. That's some character that developed, maybe because I played the part of a doctor and doctors are supposed to save lives. Maybe because I campaigned for the Equal Rights Amendment and was trying to make things better. Who the hell knows? In real life I get angry, upset, impatient. I wish people would go with who I really am."

One male movie star hates coming off as not always being wonderful, the other male movie star hates coming off as always being wonderful. We all have our façades.

When the world turns sour, your pets are still sweet. They're balm for the heart. They're the whispers from on high that let you see there is still deliciousness and sweetness and goodness in God's creatures. They're there for when life deals you a bad hand.

Research tells us animals prolong our good health. They're brought into hospitals and senior citizen homes for therapy. Whether they truly lower blood pressure or raise one from the depths, I don't know. I only know I love my babies desperately. I love those wagging tails and pleading eyes and cuddly bodies. Maybe they need me, but for sure I need them.

So I'm bewitched, bothered, and bewildered. Dazzled but frazzled. I make the soiree, but I'm not soignée. I wonder, is that what Wagnalls and his pal Funk would describe as "compromise"?

EIGHT

All Work and No Play Make a Gossip Columnist Crazy

With events calmed down in my home, my work returned to its normal panic.

Dick Cheney's office was on the phone. A lady who obviously had a poker up her panty hose screamed at me in a voice so high only dogs could hear it: "The vice president demands a retraction immediately."

"For what?"

"We demand to know your source."

"For what?"

"Mrs. Adams, I remind you we're talking about the Vice President of the United States, and we want an apology."

"For what!"

And then I realized she was talking about what I'd printed that day. Doing a column six days a week means you occasionally forget what's been published that very morning because you're out with Tuesday's column while apologizing for Monday's while writing Wednesday's while prepping Thursday's and fretting about Friday's. To lighten people's load as the world has grown harsher, I'd taken to throwing in periodic timely jokes. And my laugh for that day had been "The White House is now concentrating on the economy. Vice President Dick Cheney has told subordinates: 'The way to lick this recession is to get all those deadbeats out of the soup kitchens.'"

It was the same sort of political humor our late-night talk shows do. It, of course, had no reality behind it, no source. It was purely what it looked to be—something to make you smile. A joke. Joke. A joke. Much like what her dialogue was turning out to be.

She stridently informed me that it was no joke to them. That, in fact, they'd been inundated with calls from news agencies questioning its veracity. Veracity? And they "demanded" a retraction. Retraction?

This stupidity triggered limitless phone calls. News media wanting my "side" of the story. My editors checking in. It was a hassle. The next day, after reprising the original comment about Cheney, I printed this P.S. at the bottom of my column: "From sea to shining sea, America the Beautiful has a sense of humor. It stops at the Potomac. Washington-types wanted to know the source of my item. The Vice President's office called to deny he'd ever said it. I said, 'Of course, he never said it. It's a joke.' They wanted me to take it back. I said, I don't know how you take back a joke. So, with the music of *Les Miz* in the background, the teased-up head of c. adams is now marching to the gallows. Let it be known that, in future, Jay Leno may have to hold up cue cards saying, 'Attention D.C.: Joke coming.'"

And that was the first twenty minutes of my day. The second twenty minutes produced an irate public relations lady on the phone complaining about something innocuous on behalf of her client, actor Brendan Fraser. She was faxing his correction forthwith. It came forthwith. But so did Juicy, who picked that moment to get in touch with her inner fax dog. The fax spewed to the floor. Juicy, already on the floor, found this new mysterious toy very much to her liking. Also very tasty. By the time I wrenched it from her giant jaws, she had done a better job than those shredders at Enron. To this day I don't know what Brendan Fraser wanted me to say. But this is to tell him I loved his movie *The Quiet American* with Michael Caine and I think he's nifty and if there's ever anything I can do for him that doesn't require faxing, I'd be pleased.

Monday to Friday, my office phones ring nonstop. A houseguest once sniffed that I should consider having a phone surgically attached to my ear. Writing a column is seductive. Everyone needs something. Everyone wants something. Everyone knows a little something, even if it's only enough to win a favor in return. It can be as innocuous as the hoarse whisper: "Listen, it's Joe. Now, remember, you didn't hear this from me . . . promise you won't say I called . . . but I'm at Irving's restaurant and Richard Gere is here. And he's eating veal and spinach." Wow. Stop the presses. In return for what this caller considers a piece of gold, he will ring back two days later and want a plug for his book or art gallery or mother-in-law.

Sunday, when offices and P R people are off work, is a slow day telephone-wise. But there was this one particular Sunday when nobody called. Nobody. Not one body. Not a friend, an acquaintance, a wrong number. I have four lines. Not one rang. I plumped up the pillows behind my back. I even jiggled the receiver once to check if the phone was working.

Here I was a semi minor-key celebrity. Because of some front-page scoop I'd had, a large chunk of a morning TV program had been devoted to me. And I was watching it in bed. Alone. With the two hairy bodies tucked in with me being the loves of my life and neither bitching that I shouldn't have worn that suit jacket on the air because it made me look fat, I was blissfully happy.

After producer Marty Richards won the Oscar for *Chicago*, there were paparazzi and interviews and TV shows and flowers and fruit and candy and gifts and everyone pointing him out at parties and glad-handing and sudden requests for autographs and cameramen and flashbulbs and Catherine Zeta-Jones and Michael Douglas entering a room arm-in-arm with him and Renée Zellweger hugging him and Richard Gere and Queen Latifah shouting at him, "Marty, Marty." Came the next day. He phoned me. In tears. "When everything's said and done and you come home, it's all over. What's it all mean? You're alone," widower Marty said to me.

Me, I was totally happy. I couldn't understand those women's magazine stories about how a single person needs a companion for those dark days. Or even for those sunny ones. Or how oldish socialites should adopt youngish boyfriends because they need somethingish special in their lives. I didn't need anything. I already had those somethings special.

Jazzy Junior was maturing. Becoming quite gentlemanly, he was. When I received a phone call, he'd stop playing, trot off into a corner, sit silently like a really proper to-the-manor-born Brit from Yorkshire, and wait until I was finished. Immediately I'd hang up, he'd get frisky all over again.

Jazzy Junior was becoming a precious good-natured partner. He had a friend. A teacup named Emily who used to come and visit. Emily was aged and slow in peeing. Wherever they were when the Moment came, Jazzy Junior would wait patiently while Miss Emily the Elder did her business. Handlers said Jazzy's temperament was perfect enough for him to be a therapy dog for seniors. I said he should first specialize in his mother.

Another boy dog lived a few houses down. Jazzy was maybe becoming a little too gentlemanly. He mounted this other boy dog, whose name was Kiddo. The owner said not to worry, he's just showing domination. I said I'm not worried but I think he's a homo.

As my babies took over more of my life, I planned more of my life around them.

These two whom I'd run home to feed, whose wardrobes I'd fuss over, who shared my bed, were not animals. They were family. I wanted quality of life for them. At those times that they might otherwise have been by themselves, I began scheduling appointments at home so I could be with them. When Senator John Kerry was running for president, I had an exclusive interview booked with his wife. She was then on every front page. It was Teresa Heinz Kerry's first sit-down one-on-one, and I made it in my apartment.

First, the Secret Service came over. Early. I was schloomping around, cream on my face, nightie on my bones, my skin up in curlers, when I was informed, "The Secret Service is downstairs." We told this guy who was flashing a badge in the lobby, requesting access to my floor, to take a hike while I put some drawers on. An hour later, flashing all his ID, he came up. Very starched, he was. Very poker up his backside. Very correct. He stepped one spit-polished shoe inside my door, and Jazzy Junior pooped right on its wing toe. But smack on it. Who knew I had a Republican Yorkie?

Then I met Teresa. Nose to nose I met her. Flat out on the ground. This would-be First Lady, with whom I'd never before even exchanged a hello, arrived at my doorstep for lunch, took a look at my kids, and went down on all fours. "I've had three," came the voice of ketchup billionaire Teresa Heinz Kerry, speaking from floor level. "Rusty and Cous-cous died of old age. Rusty Two always threw up in cars. The vet couldn't cure him, and we travel so much we couldn't keep him. Now we have a German shepherd. I adore dogs."

Although *simple* and *humble* are not words often applied to Senator John Kerry's wife, my housemates cut through all the BS in seconds. The dogs were icebreakers. Juicy, who obviously likes couture, crawled right onto what nearly became the First Lap. And stayed there. What could have been a clinical interchange across an impersonal desk in some sterile borrowed office—since Teresa has no roots in Manhattan—turned fuzzy warm. We both smiled a lot. She kept cuddling my babies and kissing them. It changed the whole dynamic of our interview.

This experience emboldened me to invite an international producer over for high tea. He'd been talking about a show he thought I could do. He said he wanted me because of how important I was, how quoted I was. He also said how gorgeous I was and how talented I was. For sure, he had my attention. He came by in a stretch limo. I wasn't exactly needing to impress him, but I wasn't interested in *de*pressing him either. In the minutes it took me to give him a charming hello and usher him into my library, my whole lovely home turned into a freak show. Juicy had gotten her teeth around the end of a brand-new toilet paper roll and had rolled its total contents around the furniture and through the house. Not easy to demonstrate sangfroid and panache through a web of toilet paper.

Before the toilet paper, this producer had said how he wanted to take me to London, where he thought they'd do the filming. Sounded good. I said I'd think about it. I've had plenty of time to think about it because I never heard from him again. Whether it was me or the toilet paper, I'll never know.

I tried one more at-home gig with my babies. A TV show wanted me to opine ad nauseam on stars and their habits. Instead of my going to their nice neat pristine studio, I suggested they come to my apartment. They really wanted me to come to their studio, because it was easier for them and they didn't have to hire an outside crew. I really wanted them to put themselves out and come to me just because I wanted them to come to me. They came.

My two spoiled children were agog at the cables and cameras and equipment. They wanted to play with it all. The problem started when Juicy began eating their extension cord. The lighting man let out a yell and lunged for the cord. Juicy got scared and freaked. The lighting man got harried and fell. Smack onto an end table that featured a Ming plate. The Ming went the way of the entire dynasty. Smashed to pieces. I was horrified, (a) because the shoot had to be delayed interminably while we collected every shard of porcelain lest the babies lick it up, and (b) because it was Ming. I was so ungraciously upset that the crew, which has insurance for disasters, felt obliged to pay for its replacement. I still feel guilty about the whole incident. They'd gone out of their way to come over to my apartment. They were being so nice. It reminds me of that age-old motto: No good deed goes unpunished.

———

When God gave out great hair, long legs, patience, gentility, and the ability to do math, I was seated in the back row. However, I was right up front when it came to sectioning out guilt.

I'm big with guilt. A psychiatrist would say it's one of the things I do best. Thinking about it brings me back to when I was eight. It was the month of May. Our public school teacher had taken our class to the park for a maypole dance. Each of us, bearing a colored crepe paper streamer, wove around the maypole, one ducking under, the other going over. I wore a little dainty dimity garden party dress in aquamarine. Sash, bow in the back, puffed sleeves. I had black patent Mary Janes and white anklets.

It was strictly teachers and children. No mothers allowed. There was a black wrought-iron gate surrounding the park. This particular day my darling mother, who loved me so dearly that if she could have injected whipped cream directly into my veins, she would have, fretted that the sunny spring day might turn chilly. In the middle of our dancing, she showed up and pressed her face to the gate. She wanted to hand me a sweater.

I was mortified. At that age you want only to fit in. To be accepted as one of the pack. No other mothers had brought their children sweaters. No other mothers presented themselves to check on their "very grown-up" youngsters. Embarrassed, I turned and growled, "Go away." I feel guilty about it to this day.

In his youth my husband had been bitten by a dog, so all our years together he didn't want a pet. I felt guilty every time I threw my arms around one and snuggled it. Are you unhappy? Joey would ask me. No, I'm very happy, I'd reply. You need something else to love? No, I love you. Am I not enough for you? No, you're all that I want. Then why do you want a dog?

Guilt again.

Fade in, fade out. The years pass. My husband passes. My mother passes. Jazzy comes into my life. Jazzy takes over my life. Jazzy and his sibling *are* my life.

However . . . my job requires me to cover many events. Health codes and restaurant owners make it difficult for my doggy family to attend these parties. When they focus those sweet trusting eyes on me, I feel unhappy leaving them. So, when my editor in chief, Col Allan, and his wife, Sharon, cooked a dinner for a pack of their Australian countrymen, I was delighted that they invited me with my family. Although my kids are from Yorkshire and, thus, are Brits, it's part of the old Commonwealth. The Allans sort of felt they belonged.

Col and Sharon live in 95 percent of a Manhattan town house which includes an outdoor deck with a boardwalk-like wooden plank floor. It's where on this particular warm evening their two Maltese, named for their favorite cities—

Sydney and Manhattan, a.k.a. Syddie and Manny—and their special guests, Juicy and Jazzy, were partaking of the night air. The house's other 5 percent is the basement, which is rented to another family. Somehow, this basement is under part of their deck. How exactly this occurs, I don't know. I don't care. The architectural construction of the town house is not my problem.

What *became* my problem, however, was a rap on the Allans' door. It appeared the basement tenants were also entertaining friends. They'd placed their big bowl of greens and tomatoes and fresh mushrooms on a tabletop underneath the boardwalk slats. Seems their tossed salad suddenly needed retossing. It suddenly had a bit more dressing than they'd anticipated.

I don't care what Sharon Allan says, to this day I maintain it was Manny who lifted his leg.

Circo is a great Italian restaurant in New York. The Maccionis, who own it, love dogs. Boy, do they love dogs. One that they own is a bullmastiff. Because they're dog lovers, they allowed my entire family to have dinner in their bar area. I fretted about my New Yorkies being well behaved in this classy place, so en route, I walked Jazzy and Juicy slowly. I let them sniff every tree, fire hydrant, and storefront. When Jazzy still appeared antsy after we arrived, I took him to the ladies' room. At the same moment nature called, so did my cell. I couldn't ignore the person on the other end. It was Lindsay Lohan's father, Michael. He'd just been arrested.

Please let us not even discuss the dotty potty that flushes behind you at will. *Its* will, not yours. I whispered, "Good boy, good boy," to Jazzy, tossed in his little gift, and just as I said crisply into the phone: "I'll ring your lawyer, Dominic Barbara, immediately we hang up," the flush flushed. Such modern technology does not help my career.

I made enormous efforts to keep Jazzy and Juicy engaged. Thursdays they went for socializing. Tuesdays they went for playtime with other small dogs. It's constant playdates, so either their friends came to us or we went to them. They got walks, car rides, doggy parties, exercises in the park, plenty of air on a terrace. Trust me, Lassie didn't have such a social life.

But I live in the city, not the country, so there aren't fields around for romping. I was doing a piece on a celebrity auction. The auctioneer was an ancient curmudgeon. I should've just gone in and out, alone, quick and dirty, but instead I brought my babies with me because everything he wanted to show me was stacked in his country house. I thought, Aha! J and JJ will have country fields for romping.

Not so. It was June, and when I started out it was pleasant, but the afternoon turned hot. Very hot. My babies were panting. I brought them into the house, but it was still uncomfortably warm inside. I said to this man: "Your air conditioner is not working."

He said: "Of course it's working. Why shouldn't it be working? What makes you think it's not working?"

"Because it's not cool here."

"Well, this is the first I've heard of this. It's been working fine so far."

"So far? So far it's been winter. Air-conditioning you don't need in winter."

"The thing is brand-new."

"You told me you redid this house five years ago. Five years is not new."

"Please. It's brand-new," said this man, who had reached the age where to him five years was like yesterday. "Anyway," he said, "I don't like a lot of air-conditioning."

"A *lot*? How about a little? It's ninety degrees outside."

Because I'd ruffled him, I couldn't leave directly after we'd concluded our interview. I had to pretend to be enjoying his company awhile. He had a need to best me, so he proposed we play Scrabble. Obviously it was something at which he excelled. Fine, okay. Anything to use up an extra hour before I could gracefully take my leave. We were muddling along well, with me only slightly ahead, when he was able to place his Q on a triple-letter score. Simultaneously he pluralized a word already on the board by locking his S onto it. He surged way ahead in points.

The man sat back triumphantly, as though to say, "Go ahead now, big shot, you with your air conditioner smarts." At this exact moment Jazzy put his paw on the board and tumbled the whole thing over. Not only did this guy throw me out but he hasn't spoken to me since.

———

I loved these babies to shreds. I recognized I had to protect them even before I could protect myself *from* them. I began checking into how to take care of them if something happened to me.

A young lawyer drumming up business told me I had to meet with him and address myself to a legal document that would take care of my pets. I realized that what this was going to take care of was this lawyer. My hiring him for my problem was first going to take care of *his* problem. He said I had to make out a new will. I said, "If I make out a will for a Yorkshire terrier, who do I use as a witness? A King Charles spaniel?"

He said I had to establish a trust. A *trust*? Juicy is three pounds, three ounces. This lawyer said what I needed was to establish a legal guardian. I said what I needed was another lawyer. Legal guardian? I myself don't have a legal guardian. I don't even have a personal trainer.

He provided me with the eccentric provisions of pet lovers. One lengthy document spelled out the maintenance of a parrot. There was Danny, a three-year-old Peke who'd won Best in Show someplace and was actually accused of having a face-lift. Another dog loved Mommy's open convertible, so Mommy bequeathed money to keep the car, dog, caregiver, and see that this beloved dog was someday buried in this beloved car. And he was. They laid out the collie in the Caddy, and both were lowered into eternity.

I said I did not plan to give Jazzy or Juicy my automobile. One reason being they cannot comply with the new rules.

No matter what, they still can't dial a car phone unless it's paw held.

One testator provided a separate area be maintained in her home always for the grooming and bathing of her two Irish setters, who must be "taxied to the doctor for veterinary care." A Rockefeller left her entire New Jersey farm for the lifetime of her animals. The lawyer said I needed to leave my beauties my co-op so they might always reside at the same location. I said I didn't think our board chairman would be pleased if Jazzy and Juicy Adams voted on new carpets at the next meeting.

He showed me page three of "Statutory Protection for Dog Heirs." It states that Fido could spend his final days in a canine rest home but that this must be provided for financially because there's the rising cost of foods like "kibble quiche" and "wheat germ woofies." The document is twenty-six pages. Juicy and Jazzy need only two to poop on. What they'd do with the other twenty-four, God knows.

He said one client deposited a lump sum for the sole purpose of paying an individual so much per day for one dog's care. I told him to find something like that for *me*! Look, I love my hounds, but to work like a human just to leave enough behind to take care of two dogs whose idea of bliss is a rawhide bone seemed ridiculous. He said it's incumbent upon me to provide for a continuation of Jazzy and Juicy's existing experience. I said, What if the amount I leave is contested by his next of canine?

He said he's even seen a will that provides for chimpanzees. I said I had simple provisions, I only wanted to make sure they'd never go to the pound, and I wanted to establish a pet trust with Nazalene and her family. I didn't care whether, at their final good-bye, an orchestra played "My Country 'Tis a Tree."

I met with estate planner Herb Hummer. A nice man. He came to my home to meet my heirs. This took several sessions, but we eventually got it done. Juicy responded to my concern for her future well-being by biting off the nib of the nice man's shoelace.

I've read the will of tobacco heiress Doris Duke, who had been America's richest woman and whose legacy lives on in establishments such as Duke University. She left $100,000 to Robert. Robert was her mutt. Designer Bill Blass claimed the only organism who truly understood him was the yellow Lab Nancy Kissinger had given him. In fact, Barnaby, who'd been with Bill twelve years, was right on the bed, the master's hand on his head, when he died. Bill called Barnaby "the real love of my life."

I was not alone.

There was the day Wynonna Judd dropped by my apartment for an interview. And, trust me, that was some "drop." Large, tall, knockout-looking in full makeup featuring three shades of fire engine red (with touches of orange and yellow), hair down to the navel—you could have seen her in New Jersey. She was traveling with a troupe—publicist, agent, manager, assistant, friend, veterinarian, et cetera, plus Pixie, a teeny shivering scared puppy she'd annexed that day.

Said Wynonna: "I'm in my forties and juggling career, home, school, two children, family, health, sanity, time to love my man—and my animals. When I got married, Vera Wang made me the dress and Loretta Lynn was my flower dog."

What? Come again?

"I once had forty cats," said Wynonna. "Now it's fourteen dogs. At home in Nashville I have a thousand acres. My oldest dog, the first one I ever got, is a terrier named Loretta Lynn. Look, I love music, but dogs are my heart. Loretta Lynn's twenty. (We're talking the terrier, not the singer.) She's not well. She's on dialysis, which I myself administer personally several times a week since I'd never trust anyone else to give her the treatment.

"This dog is my life. She travels everywhere with me. I don't let anyone else tend her. When I'm on the bus on the road, she goes with me. Sleeps with me. When I'm on tour I share my bed with my kids, Elijah and Grace, and, of course, my man. And three of my dogs.

"I take Loretta Lynn everywhere. She's now arthritic, so I give her Deramaxx, a chewable beef-flavored FDA-approved drug that controls the pain of canine arthritis. See, when I was a child we Judds lived in the country. No neighbors. So Ashley and I developed a love and a need and a closeness for animals. Ashley even had birds. I actually wanted to be a vet growing up but couldn't go to school for all those years to study all the things you had to know because I'm a right brainer. I can't learn those left-brain things. But what it gave me is a love for dogs. I can't live without them."

Friends said to me: "Stop with your dogs already. Get a guy."

"Listen," I said. "You want me to do a Big Fat Geek Wedding? I don't want to get married again. Been there, done that."

"You never know," they said. "Anything could happen."

Of course anything could happen. We could be invaded by Martians. Rhode Island could declare war. I could be hit by a stagecoach. But that's not going to happen.

Today a fifth of America's electorate are single women. With living alone becoming acceptable, diverse fields now open to them, successful positions abounding, women going it solo in today's workforce have increased 30 percent. They do not necessarily pine for a husband.

Oprah's alone; Uma's alone; Whoopi's alone; Roseanne's alone; Barbara's alone; Angelina's alone; Latifah's alone; Arianna's alone; Fergie's alone; Katie's alone; Diana Ross—alone; Kim Cattrall—alone; Halle Berry—alone; Cher's alone with her Botox; Liza's alone with her lawyers; Mariah's alone with her scrapbooks; Monica's alone with her stained dress; Nicole's alone with her Oscar; Martha Stewart's alone with her spatula; Meg Ryan's alone with somebody; Tara Reid's alone during those moments she's not alone; Jane Fonda's alone—again; Pamela Anderson's temporarily alone; Charlize Theron's alone with somebody else; Cameron Diaz is legally alone but probably not for long; most of Anna Nicole Smith is alone; Kobe Bryant's wife should be alone; Joan Rivers is alone; Elizabeth Taylor Hilton Wilding Todd Fisher Burton Burton Warner Fortensky is still alone; in her last three lives Shirley MacLaine's been alone. Naomi Campbell, who leaves no man unturned, once asked me: "Do me a favor, advertise for me for a man, willya?" I told her, "Lady, you need my help like Calista Flockhart needs liposuction." Still, she's gorgeous and she's alone. Lots of ladies are alone. And plenty who are married are still alone.

And many of today's sisterhood have come to the realization that if some knight on a white charger swept them off their feet, wherever he was sweeping them he still wouldn't stop to ask directions and wherever they'd end up he'd still want to pick the movie they were going to. And however he'd want to make love, he'd leave his smelly socks on their pink pleated silk chaise. That's if he bothered to pull off those smelly socks in the first place, and if he didn't they'd sure as hell not let him even as close as the pink pleated silk chaise in the second place.

Companionship? Financial support? Hey, they can buy their own lunch. And if it's having a baby because all the glam ladies becoming mamas is the in thing and it's like having the latest Prada bag, they can do it with a dish.

Still, I thought, better these assorted bigmouths for a few hours than that one bigmouth with the smelly socks who'd live in all the time.

I was asked to participate in a documentary on the subject for the Sundance Film Festival. I told them, "I'm not alone. I have Jazzy and Juicy. Whenever I'm at work or in an office or in a stressful situation, I think about them and they make me smile."

The TV producer in the group said: "But your whole emotional stability centers around a *creature*."

I said: "In marriage the only difference is, the animal you're chained to has *two* feet.

"A husband is actually another household pet. You have to feed him and walk him. Throw him a bone now and then. Keep him on a leash. Housebreak him. Train him so he learns about gifts and anniversaries and birthdays. You even have to teach him to go potty. Maybe not 'Go on the paper' but for sure 'Don't leave the seat up.'"

"Okay, don't marry. Just find Somebody. If not for now, for later. For down the line," said another who'd been married and divorced and married and divorced.

The roundtable then came in with "Maybe down that line this Somebody won't want to stick around to spoon-feed her farina. Maybe she'll have had to put up with him all these years on spec only to have him take off when she really needs him because he found someone younger, thinner, and willinger.

"Who's to guarantee this saint she's supposed to land

will stick around when those few minutes come that she might really need him?

"What's to assure her that he won't get the call to meet his Maker before she does? You know what a waste of her efforts that would be."

The show's host said, "Meanwhile, they've wasted years. At a dinner table they sit with nothing to say to one another. On a stroll she's walking half a block in front of him. In company he puts her down with 'Again you're going to tell that story?'"

Holly, a serial divorcee, asked my opinion of great sex. I said: "How would I know? I've been married all my life."

Added Polly (and the names have been changed to protect the bitchy): "Listen, the best thing for that is a lubricant called Astroglide. So called because he then glides in like an astronaut. Comes scented and unscented."

Said Dolly: "You're in the wrong section of the anatomy. If you're really out hunting, forget the sex and go for the food. Concentrate on the guy's stomach. When you're talking forever, romance don't—cooking, do."

"Please," said Lolly. "You mean you wouldn't want Colin Farrell to do a fast jump on your bones?"

Put in Molly: "I wouldn't really mind, but afterward, there's the conversation problem. What would I have in common with Colin Farrell to talk about? I'd have to throw him out the minute—or, let's say, hour—he was finished."

Polly: "Okay, so forget Colin Farrell, how about George Clooney?"

I butted in with "First time I ever met George Clooney was in L.A. At the House of Blues on Sunset Strip. I came in with Joey Buttafuoco, who I was interviewing since he was hot in the news with his wife, Mary Jo, getting shot in the head by that teenage Amy Fisher he was having an affair with. Anyhow, so I walk in with Buttafuoco, and this big star George says to me, 'Listen, can you do me a favor? Can you arrange to get my picture taken with Joey Buttafuoco?'"

"George Clooney wanted to pose with Joey Buttafuoco?" asked someone.

"Yeah," I said.

There was a second of silence after that, followed by Polly's "Okay, so forget George Clooney. Go back to Colin Farrell."

I enjoyed my own choices. I didn't anymore want to care that some He wants a plaid bedroom. I want it pink. I didn't anymore want to care that this He wants filet of sole for dinner. I want a bacon and mayo sandwich. In bed. Reading a book. Alone. With TV, which I'm not watching but it's making a steady low rumble in the background. And what I do not want is listening to a rehash of whatever He had whined about three days before.

It set me thinking. Today's long-term marriage is three years. Prenups are based on how many weekends were spent together. Divorces get hammered out before the engagement. If betrothees split before the wedding, the protocol is she returns the ring but keeps the stone. Children are His, Hers, and the Asian sperm donor's. And wedding gifts need not be returned if the couple actually complete the ceremony.

I thought, I don't really want that. I'd rather take my chances with my dogs. Fleas are still cheaper than a matrimonial lawyer.

This lifestyle session started my sociological clock ticking again. That night, as I tried to sleep, it was another of those unwelcome visits. The Devils came knocking at the door of my consciousness.

"Who would you call?"

"Who would rush over?"

"Who would care?"

One rainy howling night the mesmerism was so thick that I said aloud, "His arms are around me, hugging me, encircling me, enclosing me, protecting me. I am not alone. God loves me." And I actually put my arms around myself.

They're robbers, those Devils. They rob your joy. They make you fret about the future. I was having to bar the door of my thought just as, if thieves wanted to steal my valuables, I would have to bar the door of my house.

The Devils danced in my brain. The world was silent, but my head was noisy.

"You're all alone."

"Nobody really cares."

"Suppose you fall . . . suppose you get sick . . ."

"If anything happens, who would know?"

"How long before someone might find you?"

I thought to myself, I really need to have a heart-to-heart with the Devils. "Look," I said to my head, "I enjoyed the luxury of privacy as an only child. I gave it up in marriage. I want it back again. I actually need it back."

"What you need is someone to love you."

"No, no, no," I told them. "A single life is the life for me. I do whatever I want whenever I want wherever I want. The older I get the less pliant my bones and my ways are. I'm not tolerant. I'm picky. A guy wears white socks, that's it. That's enough for me. I want him away from me."

But what I also wanted to tell the Devils was "Go screw yourselves."

The fact is, I love my work, I love my friends, I love my life, I love my two roommates—all I really need now is a good vacation.

NINE

Paris Is for Lovers— Dog Lovers

While there was no bird in the hand, it did look as if I was about to have a baron in the bush.

I was being romanced by a European nobleman. His mother's lineage dated back to Louis the Somebody. If not the fourteenth then, for sure at least, the eighteenth or nineteenth. We're talking a full-fledged Monsieur le Baron. I mean, if this newest charmer, who was introduced to me at a jet-set charity affair, had been born a canine, he'd have come with papers. He had all the paraphernalia. A lineage, a title, a per annum allowance, and best of all, an ancestral baronial manse in the countryside of Paris. With horses, with land, with stooped-over faithful family retainers who looked as if they predated Charlemagne.

In the words of one of my materially minded practical pals who'd seen his crest: "Marry him just for the stationery." About marrying him, I didn't know. About visiting him, I knew. Yessss!

The gentleman was sweet and utterly charming. Theoretically, his female type should have been a well-born grande dame, a natural beauty who favors small graduated pearls with twin sweater sets and more lipstick on her pinkie than on her mouth. The kind who walks around with gardening shears. Me, I do false lashes and teased hairdos. I slam on gold bangles like they're hash marks, and I never saw a pair of earrings I didn't like. But I made him laugh. Presumably, to a gentleman who sports plus-four knickers on a stroll around his grounds, a tart New Yorker is refreshing. To this tart New Yorker, whose voice has gotten played in taxis and whose face has been plastered on buses, an aristocratic European nobleman is mind-altering.

Things were nifty with me. I was happy. I was in a good place. I had lots of men friends. Brain-picking them, hearing how they think, is an enjoyable pursuit allowing total devotion since it brings strictly rewards, no penalties. Even married ones get loaned to me because I'm interested in draining them intellectually only. This single baron fell into my "friends" file.

Monsieur le Baron was very old world. When I say he was old world, I'm meaning heavy-duty old world. Didn't raise his voice, spoke ever so politely. He was in the countdown of a sticky divorce, yet it was considered an episode about which one did definitely never speak.

America's post–9/11 mentality has been a frig-the-frogs

mantra, but it's tough to turn down an invitation to Paris. As Stockard Channing put it to me when she was booked to shoot a film there: "Please, can we leave now?"

A few years earlier the late producer Ismail Merchant and director James Ivory had invited me to Paris to the set of *Le Divorce*, the movie that marked the fortieth year of their Merchant-Ivory production company. I flew in with cast member Bebe Neuwirth. Naomi Watts, Sam Waterston, and Leslie Caron were shooting in the Marais district. Ismail's welcome was a loving pat on the cheek, which schmeared ink marks all over my face. He'd been writing notes on his palm. The location was a real apartment with a real john, which the cast was using for real but which had a real problem. No toilet paper. Matthew Modine was worrying that the dark dye they schpritzed on his light hair would run in the upcoming rain scene. Someone else was asking everyone, "Anyone seen Glenn Close?"

Besides all that, the catering van for the company of sixty, with its ovens, pans, meats, and veggies, had been stolen. As a result they'd commandeered part of a neighboring café, which meant skinny health-conscious Hollywood types who usually do leaves for lunch were slogging through pork chops in gravy with fried potatoes and breaded veal cutlets snuggled into spaghetti. Instead of bottles of water, the tables had jugs of red wine. The locals were all smoking. This high-class, high-toned operation was experiencing high-quality organized chaos.

And into this mélange waltzed Kate Hudson, casually

escorting her Pomeranian. The restaurant was wall-to-wall pets, even large size, sprawled across their owners' feet. Kate told me how much she appreciated the city because dogs were welcomed everywhere. Said she: "I have three. You know, I actually went online to see what kind I might be myself. There's a dot-com quiz that tells you, basically, what kind of dog you're most like. I discovered I'm a Yorkie."

So, whereas the French may hate Americans, they love dogs.

Now, when Monsieur le Baron originally invited me to his country place, I told him, "Merci, mon ami, but I do not do country."

"Aaah, chérie, mais peut-être it is time you roughed it," he said.

Go tell someone who wears a beret that your idea of roughing it is doing without Sara Lee.

"The villa is historic," said Monsieur le Baron. "It goes back to the family of le Duc d'Orléans."

Like I cared.

"And, chérie, you may bring your dog."

Suddenly I cared. I was thrilled to be able to plop my two charges with their New Yorkie attitudes into Monsieur le Baron's fifteenth-century castle. I packed up Jazzy Junior and Juicy, and it was heigh-ho-heigh-ho, off to France we did go.

Gayle Martz, who created the Sherpa pet bag carrier, has majored in dog. I said to her, "The problem is, what if they behave like the commoners they are and christen Monsieur le Baron's Aubusson? I need lessons in how to be the proper castleguest."

"Wee-wee pads."

"I know."

"Your own personal wee-wee pads. From home."

"Why? My little mops are prejudiced? They need wee-wee pads manufactured in the USA? Trust me, they are not looking for the union label. They'll do fine with French-made stuff."

"I'm talking dirty, used, soiled ones. In fact, you have to take a really icky one along in your handbag."

"I beg your pardon?"

"In your handbag."

"In my handbag?"

"In your handbag."

Airline regulations require pets remain inside their carriers at all times and that's period, end of story. But, in case, as she explained it, they need to sneak out for a moment and need to go, clearly we could not have Monsieur Jazzy lifting his leg against fellow passenger Madame Jolie's leg. Plan B would be to carry her/him/them in their bag to the lav, fling down that familiar junky ratty smelly wee-wee Chux, let them sniff and circle, and bingo! Those used peed-on pads were insurance.

The airfare was ninety dollars per dog. Why I don't know, since they neither eat nor drink and rarely watch the movie. And there's so much paperwork. They have to be microchipped and freshly vaccinated against assorted dis-

eases. They need health certificates, veterinarian documentation, a shot record, rabies blood work from a central lab. I
had a bulging folder plus a stamped numbered official tag
certifying they'd been physically checked within one week
of departure and were found 100 percent A-OK. The air-
lines demanded it. The travel agents demanded it. The
French authorities demanded it. Two dogs in heat in Alsace-
Lorraine demanded it. Fearful that the authorities would
find some fault and that they'd not be allowed on board or,
worse, wrenched from me and placed in cargo, I carefully
carted my bulging "Jazzy and Juicy Folder" tucked into the
waistband of my panty hose to the check-in counter.

Nobody asked for anything. Nothing. Zippo. I could've
had a Saint Bernard with the mange for all anybody cared.
All they wanted was the price of the doggy ticket.

Jazzy and Juicy had a whole set of bags. It was wee-wee
pads, bulging folder, chew toys for the trip, squeaky plush
toys for after they arrived. Then, because I doubted they
were into haricots verts and escargots, I had to pack wet
food, dry food, treats. Medications in case they had tummy
trouble. Since they'd be on display, I needed extra collars
and matching leashes. In case they wanted to hike the Bois
de Boulogne, I needed halters and extension leashes. It was
winter, so they had to have coats. For the plane trip, little
sweaters.

I took their food bowls, water bowls, favorite blankets,
because who knew how drafty a castle with a moat is. They
needed their soft-sided easy totes, the ones I use for schlep-

ping them around town. And their tiny collapsible water cups. God, I was so busy with them, and together they're only seven and a half pounds. I hadn't even taken this much gear for myself. And when you're talking about *my* weight . . . Let's not go there.

Nazalene had packed a special travel kit—his 'n' hers paper towels in case, and treats because I doubted they'd go for the stale cashews the airline served. I had an eighth of a quarter of a doggy Dramamine each, which the vet said would calm them if noise or turbulence or some pest sitting next to me with the croup upset them. And I had pieces of American cheese in which to roll up and hide the doggy Dramamine so I could stuff the things down them.

The supervisor directly inside the airport entrance recognized me. Louis his name was. "It isn't classy for such an elegant famous lady to be hauling all of this to the counter yourself," he said. "Allow me," he said.

I was grateful, but I didn't want to trouble him. "Please," he said. "Do not offend me. I my very own personal self am going to take care of you." I loved this man. He put my bag in a carton for security. Sealed it. Gift-wrapped it. Put stickers all over it. Printed my name on the outside with a felt pen. Did all but lock it in a chastity belt. I thought, Monsieur le Baron should only treat me this well.

Such a nice man. He wouldn't accept any tip. "No, it's my pleasure," he said. "I read you every day. I love your column. I enjoy you on television. I'm delighted to meet you in person. Please accept this little bit of service as my gift."

That made me feel good, but then, I nearly had a coronary when some new draconian security measure called for shrink-wrapping each little animal in its carry bag, punching holes in the top so it could breathe, and securing the thing in the cabin out of reach so each of you has zero access to one another until you're through customs. Plastic-wrapping my Juicy? Right away I thought, Houston, we have a problem. I planned to tell them they could take the crest, the trip, their whole country, and the Baron and shove it and I was not going when, for whatever reason, they backed off on it.

My usual travel gear includes a hat, because who needs to worry how the hair looks? And a jacket with a blouse underneath because, temperature-wise, who knows if I'll be hot or cold? I don't like using the airline blankets. God knows who coughed or sneezed in them. This way, if I'm chilly, I keep the jacket on. In the old days this worked. Now, forget it. Security made me take off my hat in case I had a machete under it, which meant from the neck up I looked like a Zulu. Then they said, Off with the jacket, since they had to check to be sure there wasn't some AK47 hiding in my navel. I wore a sleeveless shell under the jacket. My buff bod was thus framed in two upper arms, which were I to wave good-bye, would stop waving ten minutes later. You could get a concussion. Put it this way, I haven't looked at my upper arms in twelve years. Even in the shower I wear long sleeves.

Next to go at the metal detector was my belt with the

carved silver buckle. And shoes. Unfortunately, because I was traveling with two dogs and everyone was cootchy-cooing them, I was attracting more stares than normal. Also unfortunately, the nail of my big toe was poking through my stocking. Huddled in the middle of an airport on the equivalent of a really bad hair day with arms that look like Merkel hams, legs in beltless pants that were then puddling, and stockings with holes in them is not an attractive experience. I was already cursing the baron.

And then, they confiscated my tweezer. My brand-new favorite. Pink colored, it was. With a razor-sharp slanted bottom. Hand-selected for me by Mr. Dal LaMagna, who owns Tweezerman.

I explained: "Without that I will soon look like Abe Lincoln."

No response.

I pressed on. "We are not speaking of everyday old cockamamie tools. We are talking the Tiffany of pliers. These could uproot a hundred-year-old palm tree."

Nothing.

I pleaded with the security man. I explained I could handle many hardships. A zit on my chin. A Yorkie with diarrhea. A guy who cheats, which I almost don't even mind because that's like take-out food—less work for Mother. Give me liberty or give me death, but give me mostly my tweezer, I said.

Sighed a fat guy who seemed to be in charge, "Lady, we're not taking your citizenship. Only the tweezer."

"How will it help fight terrorism if I turn into a chimp?"

"You can have that instrument only if you stick it in your luggage."

"My luggage is already checked." The lone alternative, which I suggested, was to give this valuable instrument to the pilot. They said uh-uh. Okay, then how about Scotch-taping it to the belly of the plane? They said no.

The guards eventually schlepped me to a special area and examined me like I was Mrs. bin Laden. To tell you the truth, if I had to go forever without tweezing, I too, would have gone under the veil.

And there's the picture-ID problem. That means either driver's license or passport. Years ago I did a book on the Gabors—Mama Jolie and her daughters Zsa Zsa, Eva, and Magda. I learned then that the Gabors' true age could be determined only by the rings around their gums. They even had their documents face-lifted. I personally believe they went to some birth certificate surgeon in downtown Budapest. As I reluctantly, angrily handed over my picture ID, I wondered how the Gabors would've handled it if they were around traveling today.

Anyway, armed with dogs and tons of carry-on, I got all but a cavity search. Probably the only reason they didn't make me strip naked and assume the position in the middle of the airport was there was no proctologist on duty who'd majored in security.

Nowadays you have to get all puffed and fluffed before you make a plane trip. You need a pedicure because the shoes come off. A blow-dry because the hat comes off. A personal trainer because the jacket that hides everything comes off. And from the exertion of carrying your own stuff and hurling and stuffing and pushing the handheld luggage and hoisting it to the overhead bin, a person also ends up sweating. Thus, an extra added attraction to my already stunning composition was rings of perspiration around the armholes. I tried to keep my arms down, which made it hard when I had to lift the sacks with the dogs. I wondered if the baron ever did carry-on.

And that's the menu before you hit the wild blue yonder. That window seat is a bitch. Any cameraman will tell you, overhead lighting shows every line, pore, crack, shred of fuzz, discoloration, imperfection, and pencil line where a perfect arched brow should have been. Bright sun glances off the makeup, which looks like Day-Glo 35,000 feet up. It's three words. For-get it. Yet that's where I had to sit so my babies could stay tucked away and not bother some allergic dog hater across the aisle.

Eventually I, this high-class baroness in waiting, boarded the plane, bearing a Lana Marks alligator tote in which were stuffed slices of cheese in a plastic Baggie, plus two peed-on/pooped-on/crapped-on/wee-weeed-on wee-wee pads. Boy, did I not smell like Chanel No. 5. I smelled more of number two.

They'd never flown before. Juicy is cool, but I worried Jazzy would be a white-paw flier. I collected all his health certificates—vaccination, parvo, rabies, the shot record of every inoculation he'd ever had, including when we knocked him out to clean his teeth. Vice President Cheney didn't have such medical documentation.

By the time I folded myself into the seat, I was exhausted. Requiring some pick-me-up to keep me alive, I asked the flight attendant for a second pack of nuts. The strange passenger next to me, who it seemed did not ingest salt, said, "Wow, you can sure pack it away." Not the most flattering thing you ever heard.

I was busy the entire flight. I had the babies lick ice cubes so they wouldn't dehydrate because they couldn't be given water or they'd have to go to the powder room. I fed them the infinitesimally small tranquilizers inside their pieces of cheese. I reached in and petted them. I snuck them bits of snacks. They were well cared for, so they were fine. I was so busy caring for them that I wasn't.

Seven hours later, when we arrived, I was knocked out. The dogs' cases came off promptly. My single case, not. I hung around the empty baggage carousel for so long my pantsuit went out of style. My bag, using its frequent flier mileage, was definitely making a longer trip than I was. For all I knew, it was inside the cargo bay of some antique Fokker in Munich. Like our friendship with France, it had vanished.

The baggage master gave me an 800 number to call and told me the 800 number is "our airline's personal service to reclaim lost luggage. They'll take care of it for you." I dialed so often that I had no middle finger left to raise if ever I saw

Louis again. Ultimately, a nice gentleman with a slightly Indian lilt responded and took my pertinent information. Somehow I didn't feel secure, so hours later I rang again. This time a different voice. However, the sound, inflection, speech patterns were the same. Dozens of calls over two days reached other persons, all of whom sounded like they were from New Delhi. "You in the United States?" I asked.

"No."

"France?"

"No."

"Europe?"

"No."

Replied the twentieth voice: "India."

"You mean," I asked, "I flew New York to Paris and I'm phoning India for my luggage?"

"Yessir," said the voice.

Fly an American carrier. Call India for your car sack.

The January weather was unseasonably hot. I'd come prepared in thick coat, fur mitts, bulky turtlenecks, fleece-lined boots. It was one degree in New York when I packed. It was forty in Paris when I arrived. The plane had been overly warm. My traveling ensemble was now Krazy-Glued to my bones. The thing could only have been removed via surgery. I was so warm that my armpits were growing mold. The moisture fortunately didn't show because it was raining daily.

On Day Two I accidentally dropped my lipstick on my pants. My *only* pants. Besides looking like a poster child for

Send This Girl to Camp, I now had a red blotch around my lap.

The streets were full of Dior and Chanel, but that's heavy-duty prices and the euro is not favorable to the dollar and each morning I figured my lost bag, thanks to Louis, was coming that day.

I'm a puffy size six. One American in Paris friend who'd lost twenty pounds down to size 12 said, "I just bought a suit here. Blue. Not expensive, but so what? I never put it on. You can wear it if you like."

Designer Vicky Tiel, who shows at Bergdorf Goodman in New York and has a boutique on the Left Bank, had something marvelous the equivalent of size 10. She said, "If you don't mind hiking up the sleeves or doubling up the skirt, you can borrow whatever you want." She also directed me to a young, hip lingerie boutique along Ile St.-Louis. The stuff was too snappy for my various parts. Silk teddies are for people who are definitely doing better work than I am.

Eventually the luggage arrived, and it was off for the three-day visit to Monsieur le Baron. His aged Mercedes collected us and chugged us into an area surrounded by hundreds of acres. Juicy, who was sitting up front, did something I'd never seen before. An hour out, with nothing to look at save bushes upon unrelieved bushes, she actually cemented her paw on the steering wheel. She was getting in touch with her inner bored dog. After that she did it each time we took another ride along that same terrain. It was her way of saying: "Enough already with this endless drive." Juicy should have been a tour guide. She knew tiresome when she saw it.

In New York the Baron had explained, "You just fly to Paris and my villa is right there." Yeah? Lotsa luck. What was "right there" was this ancient touring car with a bud vase and a road from the Paris airport that took four and a half hours to navigate. This was followed by a twenty-minute drive through his property to the front door. Boy, did my pal the Baron not get drop-ins. Even Stanley and Livingstone couldn't have found this place.

The grounds opened to a tree-lined hidden driveway that wended and wound along forever. It led to an entrance great hall rife with art. Forget Peter Max prints. The wall hangings were antique tapestries by van Eyck.

Everyone around was a hyphenate. The chauffeur was Jean-Claude, the geezer valet Jean-Pierre, the footman Jean-Marc. There was Jean-Louis, Jean-Phillippe, Jean-Marie, Jean-Georges, and Jean somebody else. And all the shopping bags in all the dusty cavernous armoires said Hermès or Vuitton.

We are not talking a Hilton here. We are talking a castle. To trigger the generator, you had to switch on at least two lamps at the same time. Unless you rubbed two locals together, there wasn't enough juice to charge your cell. You went to the can at night via flashlight. Jazzy didn't know how to work the flashlight, so he found my slippers.

The telephone worked no week that had a Tuesday in it. No message service, no answering machine. Also not much sound. If you weren't tethered to the hard-wired cord, you didn't hear the thing ring if, in fact, the thing actually rang. You received a call on this rotary phone by prearrangement. That meant you had to make the initial call to tell the caller what time they should call so you'd be there when the old-style heavy black instrument rang. There was no hold button. And no extension. You physically had to be alongside the main instrument when the phone call came in. Perfect for someone employed in the news business, right?

The first day it rained. The gas went out. The stove went poop. So my morning coffee went south. And some ratty little gnat bit me where I sit. Possibly I should have been grateful. It had been years since any living creature took a bite out of my behind.

The place also had, what seemed to my city mind, loons. As in crazy as a loon and laughing like a loon. One night when the stillness was deafening I couldn't sleep for the silence. At 1:30 my Jazzy went ape. He yelped nonstop and careened crazily up and down the hallway. He scratched at the door. I got up. He was running around, and I was running after him with a flashlight.

With Jazzy leading the charge, we toured the surrounding forestry. Nothing. I figured in the stillness he must've heard a pinecone drop and the noise upset him. My host had confided that the word was the castle was haunted. Two decades before he'd seen a soldier in a uniform with gold buttons carrying a musket. I wanted to tell him what I wanted to see was a yellow cab carrying me.

Cold and shivering, we lumbered back. My hound slept perfectly with garbage cans clanking, horns honking, and taxis crashing. He was used to Avon ladies knocking, not feral raccoons foraging. Mighty Dog wasn't doing well in the rustic outdoors.

Came 4:30 and Jazzy woke us again. Again it was some wildlife sound. Jazzy began baying again. Again it sounded as if it might have been something like a loon. I wouldn't 100 percent have known, because I'd never actually come up against a loon before. That is, they may come up on our apartment building's service elevator but not outside my window.

The second night the phone tinkled. It was my editor calling from back in civilization. Two seconds after I said "Hello" the contraption that Alexander Graham Bell himself must've used cut out. Thinking I was a normal person in a normal environment my editor hollered: "I'll ring you again." That meant I had to sit there. I couldn't leave that room.

I explained to my host, who had pattered down in slippers and was standing there patiently, "In terms of family, I'm fine with Father Christmas, but Mother Nature just doesn't do it for me."

"Perhaps, ma petite, you might call the gentleman back," he said.

Like I could. There was no way to hand-crank it.

Sleep was not something my wired hound was about to do, so I spent the rest of the hours until dawn rummaging around the bookcase. I was thrilled to find a newspaper. It was a *Le Figaro* job from July 4, 1967. The headline? If deciphered correctly: U.S. MARINES HURL BACK VIET CONG THRUST.

The phone again.

"Here's what we need you to do," crackled the editor. "Get the hhyettwgw . . ."

"I can't hear you. Do what?" I shouted.

"Check with them and fhympysanndy . . ."

"You're breaking up. Repeat. Do what?"

Click.

Two dogs lived in. One, a standard poodle. Black, male. The other an Afghan. They do not sit on laps. If anything, you might sit on theirs. To them mes petits chiens were hors d'oeuvres. Bite-size.

In summer the 2:30 P.M. daily entertainment was croquet. On the lawn. The Baron always wore an ascot. I thought of the first man in my life. Boy, was my husband's designated afternoon sport different. Joey and his low-rent pals used to play an urban street-style baseball called stickball. Joey was known as a two-sewer man. He could swat the length of two sewers.

Dinner was formal attire. It was right out of a B-movie English drawing room comedy. Proper suit and tie for the gents, long dress for the females. Tank tops and cutoff jeans could send you to the guillotine. As for our sleeping arrangements, Monsieur le Baron occupied the entire third floor's dozen rooms. I was confined to the second floor, from which I was not to move after 10:30 because the alarm with its motion sensors was preset.

Monsieur le codger did not know how to deactivate the timed motion sensors, and I thought it unladylike to crawl on my belly under the radar. That was strictly something Denzel Washington might do. So at 10:30 it was candles out. If J and JJ wanted to creep downstairs late at night for a romp or a bone-shaped croissant, forget it. The lone sounds after 10:31 were the gurgling johns. The plumbing was not cutting edge American Standard. The water closets could gurgle forever.

I, however, could not. The thought came that three days was, possibly, the length of my entire future with this really terrifically charming baron.

I truly was enamored of this elegant gentleman, whose background I could not share. Nor could I share many of my smart Manhattan-born anecdotes with the one lone guest, a countess who was his neighbor and who had a hearing aid and who sat in the middle of this dinner table the length of a football field with the Baron at one end and myself at the other and giant silver candlesticks in the middle. Neither one of them was particularly interested in my shouting my repertoire of Rudy Giuliani stories, on which I have often dined out. At one point I mentioned Toni Morrison, and Madame la Comtesse asked politely: "And who might he be?"

There was also the matter of the food. Exquisitely served. Just not pressed down and running over. I am a knife and fork pro. An eater whose mouth should be equipped with a coin-operated zipper. I'm not into a lottery to determine who wins the last see-through slice of veal.

And there was the matter of the Baron's great-great-great-grandfather's suit of armor. One morning, after a long trot outdoors, Jazzy Junior, Juicy, and I raced straight to their powder room, whereupon Juicy tour jetéd three inches to the left and let go on the Baron's great-great-great-grandfather's suit of armor. Ah, well, to err is human, to forgive canine. I fretted only lest the thing rust before I could get a coach and horse out of there.

There was yet one additional matter. It came to fruition as I was dressing to attend some soiree at a nearby art gallery. Our invitation was for six o'clock. It was then five o'clock. Monsieur le Baron was already set to leave because, as becomes him, he is proper and respectful. The dying breed who will never be late. In fact, he prefers being early. In fact, very early. Always early. Everywhere early. I learned the man gets to airports before the pilots get their wake-up call.

I say, "But events are never on time. An advertised 6:00 P.M. showing means 6:30 minimum."

"Cannot be sure, my dear," he said. He'd been ready since 4:15.

"I'm sure," I said.

Fifteen minutes later, as I was spitting on the mascara, he'd moved from his previous post near the front door and was peering at his wristwatch. "I'm getting accustomed to waiting for you." He smiled. I smiled back. I thought: If he wouldn't start three hours in advance, he wouldn't be waiting.

The man had now placed himself inside my lipstick tube. Seeing him at the edge of the dressing table, I realized I did not want him there. I did not want him at my dressing table or anywhere else. What I wanted was for him not to be anyplace. What I wanted was for him not to be. Gone was what I wanted him. And why? What was this sin he had committed? To shuck off a really fine gentleman because he's a little overly punctual is to admit you're not totally sane. So I realized there must be something wrong with me, but the simple fact is—me I had to live with. Him I didn't.

My little babies were not yet international cosmopolites, and I was a mother who wanted the best for them. It was now time for Monsieur Jazzy Junior and Mademoiselle Juicy to move into the city proper and do the Champs-Elysées.

Whether it was because of the economy, the airline security, or the post-9/11 lack of U.S. tourists arriving and spending, suddenly the Parisians were downright almost semipolite. My friend the actress Line Renaud, explained, "Chérie, France and America are like lovers. Always fighting but always together."

When asked why his people don't like the Americans, one French ambassador sighed to me, "Madame, the French don't even like the French."

But they did adore the dogs. Theirs—President Jacques

Chirac's favorite Christmas gift was a white doghouse for his bichon frise Sumo—and mine. Everyone fussed over my babies. I was told they were welcome everywhere, therefore I took them everywhere.

There was dinner at Fouquet. I arrived with J and JJ hidden in my shoulder bag. They smelled food and began speaking up.

The maître d' said, "Your sac is barking, madame."

"May I take the dog out?"

"Of course, Madame."

"It's *two* dogs."

"Of course, Madame." The maître d' then presented a moth-eaten wallet photo of his own beloved pug.

Next night at L'Orangerie, I asked permission to take them out of their bag.

"Please, madame," they said. "We love dogs." The owner then brought a bowl of specially cut up beef and veggies. They dined right at my foot.

At lunch at Le Procope, the two actually sat on my lap and drank water from my stem glass. The patrons nearby smiled.

Sitting on the elegant velvet chair alongside me, they shared my omelette at the Hotel Bristol dining room. At LaSerre, whenever some specially tasty charcuterie passed by, they'd whine. They hit C over high C. I worried my host would be asked to leave, but nobody minded. The nearby diners just raised their voices. Not their eyebrows, their voices.

At a patisserie the clerk bent down to gave them a lick

off his finger of whipped cream. At a bistro I ordered an extra portion of chicken to take home for them. The management didn't even charge for it.

Maybe my loving two little Yorkies made me seem nicer in the eyes of the Parisians. Maybe they showed the unexpected vulnerability of someone from the United States instead of the expected arrogance. Possibly their smiles were a mirror of what they suddenly saw reflected in me, I don't know. Dr. Tom Haggai, a minister, claims we can learn from dogs. His mantra about us humans is, "When your loved ones come home, always run to greet them . . . dance around, wag your entire body . . . and avoid biting when a simple growl will do."

These dogs became my teachers. Because of them I experienced my first-ever Parisian smiles. Except at one classy boutique along rue du Faubourg St.-Honoré. The mademoiselle snipped, "Put zem in ze bag." I put zem in ze bag.

My babies adapted well to the trip. No nervous submissive puddles. No jet lag. No hang-ups with their diet. They loved French bread, French cheese. I looked into their eyes, their ears, their faces, their souls daily. One morning I went shopping with Monsieur le Baron and all I bought were heart-shaped red hot-water bottles. Each said "Paris" on it. These objects were perfect to stick under the doggies' beds in cold weather because they were flat and small and wouldn't lump up the beds. The outside skins were heavy jelly, thus very protective. I bought six. That's what I brought from Paris. Six hot-water bottles for my dogs.

I'd truly become a member of the Pathetic Pet People's

Club. I knew always to feed them before myself, but one evening, all mixed up with the change of time, I was hungry. However, it was not their proper mealtime. They'd just had their late afternoon mini raw carrot treat, and it was too early for their dinner. But, Pathetic Pet Person or not, I was starving. There were lots of goodies in the apartment in which we were staying. The problem was, how could I gobble it in front of them? They'd sniff food. They'd want food.

I did the only intelligent thing. I threw off my robe and slippers, got all dressed, dragged myself down to the brasserie two blocks away in the pouring rain, and had a sandwich rather than deal with it.

On the way home I bought a mango. I love mangoes. They're my favorite fruit. I brought it back, and just as I put the key in the door, the phone rang. Nazalene, who missed us all—mostly the babies, "her" babies as she calls them—calling from home. She knows my habits, my likes and dislikes, so I said to her, "Naz, guess what I found here? A mango. I can't wait to taste it."

Said Nazalene: "Don't eat it all. Give some to the babies."

My housekeeper, my mango, my Jazzy Junior and Juicy were all sweet. Life was good. Two days later I kissed Gay Paree and the Baron bye-bye—the better to see both again soon—packed up my babies, hot-water bottles, and dirty wee-wee pads, and flew home.

Paris may be for lovers, but New York is where my heart is.

$\mathcal{L}$ife and $\mathcal{C}$indy's $\mathcal{A}$partment $\mathcal{A}$re $\mathcal{W}$orks in $\mathcal{P}$rogress

 My babies had seen boutiques open in Jazzy's name—Jazzy, the Park Avenue Dog—in Macy's, Saks Fifth, Ritz Hotels. Entertainment outlets like Larry King, E! Entertainment, *E.T.*, *The View*, the *Today* show, Animal Planet, *People* magazine, *Star* magazine, *Vanity Fair*, *Good Housekeeping*, *New York Post*, the Sunday *Times*, *The Christian Science Monitor*, *USA Today*, *Cosmo*, *Reader's Digest* all had featured my dogs. Some played up their friends, like Bryant Gumbel with his six-pound Maltese, Cujo, and Mary Tyler Moore, who lugged Shayna, her rescue poodle, to Jazzy's birthday party. There was Henry Kissinger, who apologized for coming to one event for Jazzy without his hound "because he is in duh country." He arrived at the same time as Susan Lucci, who'd brought her aging snow-white powder-puff bichon frise plus her daughter's Lab, Charlie, who's the size of a Buick and, at ninety-

eight pounds weighs more than Susan. And writer Amy Tan, carrying two teacup Yorkies in twin matching bags. And Mary J. Blige, Chazz Palminteri, Bill Clinton, Erica Jong. I'd been selling Jazzy Couture clothes on QVC.

Jackie Collins, whose recipe for smarmy best sellers about Hollywood wives, Hollywood husbands, Hollywood kids, probably even Hollywood hookers is sex, scandal, sex, drugs, sex, power, sex, money, sex, divorce, and daisy petals dictating "Screw me, screw me not," said to me, "Enough with the dogs. You need a man."

I told her Jazzy and his sister, Juicy, were my live-ins. My family. My only blood relatives. They slept with me. They cuddled me. They warmed my feet on a cold night. I never had dinner alone. When I wanted to go for a walk, they were company. Neither argued with me. Didn't give me in-law problems. I told her not only did we blend into each other but we were one unit. I didn't want any other warm body living in.

What I knew for a fact was that animals don't mess with you like people do. But I reckoned without Joan Collins's sister, who had started early. Born of a theatrical family, knowing showfolk since cradlehood, having an older movie star sister, she met a sailor in the south of France at thirteen, was expelled from school at fourteen, dated Marlon Brando at fifteen, and was temporarily married to a drug addict.

Said Jackie: "I know it all, and I think you need a man to live with you. But forget actors. They're too much into themselves. And avoid Australians unless your bones just need a quick jump start. They're sexy but not faithful. And stay away from movie execs. They're pigs. Accustomed to having everything—if not everyone."

Jackie smiled through capped teeth. "Darling, barring two poodles in Beverly Hills, I know the habits of every bitch in Southern California. And I tell you, if you're man shopping, the movie capital is not the place. The women are all young. Competitive. Eager to get someplace—other than under those sheets. They'll do everything."

Understated Jackie, who features wall-to-wall twenty-two-karat gold earrings, necklace, pin, buckle, rings, bracelets, and probably fillings, has rooted around in all of the Hollywood ladies' past lives. She has enough dirt for a landfill off the end of Malibu. With her the message to me was simple: "Look for a man in New York."

I told her Jazzy was the only male I wanted.

Other specialists came in with hand-tailored advice. Dr. Joyce Brothers, who'd earlier touted me off CEOs, told me that just in case I was in the market for a lover, the absolute worst are scientists. "They're too busy experimenting with other things. Doctors are bad, too, because they never have enough time. And athletes strike out because, with their exercise schedule being elsewhere, they're usually too wound up or used up."

Said Dr. Brothers: "The dream lover is a clergyman. Parsons, deacons, rabbis, reverends, chaplains embody components that make for good, warm, loving human beings."

You mean, I asked, that in terms of actual technique, men of the cloth really make superior lovers?

"Top of the list. They're accustomed to being unselfed. They're gentle, tender, and giving. Their masculinity is not threatened by adjusting to another's needs. They're not un-comfortable at subordinating themselves to their fellow man—or woman."

I appreciated Dr. Brothers trying to be helpful, but the truth was, in 2002 I was a bridesmaid at the Liza Minnelli–David Gest wedding. The ceremony lasted longer than their union. Michael Jackson, whose own personal life is pretty interesting, and Elizabeth Taylor Hilton Wilding Todd Fisher Burton Burton Warner Fortensky, who knows a few things about weddings, were co–ring bearers. Another marriage vet, Gina Lollobrigida, whose wig obscured the first three pews, was also a bridesmaid. Donald Trump, Rosie O'Donnell, Sir Anthony Hopkins were among the eight million guests. Natalie Cole sang. Robert Wagner, part of the bridal party, kept whispering, "At rehearsal we were told to enter stage right." Stage right? It was a church.

The bride and groom pledged undying love. They kissed. They hugged. They got it on national TV. A year later they were suing one another for battery and lying and stealing—and those were just the nice parts.

So, sometimes the red-hot human-to-human adoration doesn't last—but at all times the love between you and your pets does.

Jazzy and Juicy cared for me. A few days before Jackie's pronouncements, we'd all navigated the park along the Upper West Side's Riverside Drive. It's hilly. Deep steep stairs from the street level down to the waterfront. I was in heels. I had to negotiate the steps sideways. Slowly. Clutching the railing. Jazzy bounded down until before the end of the leash played out, then waited calmly for me to catch up. When I was a step away, off he scampered again. Then he found another landing and waited patiently for me, his eyes searching mine. I said to him, "Pal, in another life you must've been trained in a nursing home." It was clear we watched out for one another. We cared for one another.

I had in fact reached the point where I was tailoring my social life around my babies. A couple I knew slightly, the Gourdones, were having a formal gala in their apartment. I would never have gone ordinarily, but it was to celebrate the thirteenth birthday of Pom Pom, their girl Pomeranian, and people were invited with their dogs. It was a lousy night weather-wise. Raining, blowing, windy. I'd allowed extra time to slosh through the streets, so my brood and I arrived exceptionally early. Too early for a crowd to be going up in the elevator. When the doorman announced us, I noticed a bit of hesitancy. He stared at me and shuffled his feet while nattering away on the house phone. Finally he said, "Well, you may go up."

Because it was a typhoon outside and I knew this glamorous playdate would keep us there awhile, I sent Reggie off to get some hot soup and told him to be back in two hours. Jazzy, Juicy, and I arrived barking and yipping at the appointed floor. Cuddled into their doorway amid a terrifying silence were two sleepy people. Mr. and Mrs. Gourdone. In pajamas. Rubbing their eyes. "Are we *that* early?" I asked.

"No, late," she said.

"Late?"

"The bark mitzvah was last week."

What was left of my mind began racing. Reggie was already MIA. I began burbling. I suggested the doorman get us a cab. They called downstairs, but no cabs. There was a long line waiting of them. Even Sadie Thompson had never seen such rain.

Standing smack in the center of their living room, my puppies shook themselves vigorously. Pools eddied out from under the hosts' pink and beige Aubusson.

I couldn't get out of there. I was trapped. And they were trapped with me. And they knew it. There was no way to get rid of either me or their freshly energized Pomeranian. I'd waked them from a sound sleep, and now they were stuck with us, and Jazzy and Juicy were sloshing through their house, tearing after Pom Pom.

The rainwater off my shoes had settled around one gilt leg of a Louis Quatorzeish chair. But Mr. Gourdone hadn't settled. He was still standing there. And Mrs. Gourdone was racing after the Pomeranian, who was crazed as a result of her drop-in guests. I tried to defuse the situation, but there's a limit to how far "Oh, isn't Pom Pom cute with my two puppies?" will go. A slight silence settled over the room once that subject ground to a halt.

I reached for my cell, but I was too nervous. I couldn't find it. What my hand came up with were treats, which dribbled onto the already damp Aubusson. I *had* to find Reggie. Still wearing my wet coat, I flopped across the Gourdones' low coffee table like a beached whale and clawed at their telephone. I hadn't the number of our garage, and my car wasn't responding. What was responding was a newly exercised Yorkie. Jazzy had brought a slobbery ball into this salon which the week before had been the lone room that was closed off to the doggy guests. And jazzy was showing off in front of Pom Pom. He'd perfected a new trick which he'd never had seven minutes earlier. He was hurling his entire body at me, jumping up on his hind legs, and butting me. We're talking torture. I'd have sold one of my arms to get out of there.

Eventually I located Reggie at his favorite deli. With a pastrami sandwich still handing from his mouth, he came for me. A good quarter of an hour of forced charm later, my dogs and I mercifully got out.

Jazzy and Juicy and I were in sync. I understood their rhythms. We'll go out. I'll stash them in their carry bag. One block down the street, Jazzy will whine. I know what he's telling me. That means he wants out. Jazzy loves to walk. Juicy's legs, however, are shorter than my eyelashes. A marathon to her is one lap around the apartment. Halfway along one street and it's her turn to whine. I know what she's telling me. She wants to be carried. I understand all that. We were all very together.

Juicy will drop a toy on my chest to rouse me in the morning. First, she'll wake up, stretch her front paws, stretch her back paws, scoot her tushy, rub and roll her full body along the quilt, then stand at attention right next to one of my body parts. Usually something about this routine wakens me. But if not, if I'm feigning sleep or there's legitimately no response from my dead-to-the-world bones, she has no compunction. Also no patience. Also no respect. She'll walk right onto me—onto my chest, stomach, neck, or forehead—whichever of my parts she selects. She will then drop a toy right on it.

That is my ultimate final cue. It means, "Enough already. I want attention. How long am I supposed to dance attendance on you? Pick yourself up?" And up I pick myself. Yes, we are all very together.

Jazzy, on the other hand, will play hard to get. He'll stand on the edge of the bed. I'll reach out for him. He'll run away. I'll lie back again. He'll come again. He'll stand on the edge of the bed again. I'll reach out for him again. He'll run away again. It's ballet. Each of us does her or his part. He will next inch a bit closer. I will ignore him. He will then circle me. I will nail him. He will then allow me to cuddle and kiss and ruffle and smooch him. Even when I bite his ears, he will pretend not to notice. He will be looking away. Off in the distance. Each of us is well choreographed.

Juicy also doesn't like gratings. Subway gratings. Gratings covering cellars of whatever they're covering. She stops dead when the tar or cement sidewalk turns to a metal screening. She won't budge. Not a step, not the length of half a paw. I live on Park Avenue, which is considered one of Manhattan's nicer sections. It's built over a railroad line. Thus, it's got gratings everywhere. So what? Who cares? Only Juicy. She sees her brother walk over them. I walk over them. Her animal pals in this city walk over them. Juicy, not. I have crawled hand in hand, knee to knee alongside her, encouraging her as, mother and daughter, we could traverse a six-inch-wide nonthreatening panel of metal mesh somewhere. No. She won't. So, if necessary, she can get picked up eight times on one block.

Jazzy is okay with walking anywhere. He's interested only in getting attention. Trust me, Kevin Federline doesn't pet his missus, Britney Spears, as much as I pet Jazzy. A colleague brought over a long-haired Chihuahua for a playdate. This delicious little girl Chihuahua's name was Fluffernutter. The name was bigger than the dog. She and Jazzy, whose tail was wagging big-time, were playing happily—chasing, fetching, sniffing. I made the mistake of reaching down to put Fluffernutter on my lap and cuddle her. Jazzy could've become governor of California. In two seconds he turned into the Terminator. He growled. His legs took an aggressive stance on the floor. His eyes locked onto

her. The tail stopped wagging. I quickly put our visitor
down. He nipped her. He went back as though to really bite
her nose off. I grabbed Fluffernuttter and placed her out of
harm's way. I knew enough not to aggravate Jazzy.

A mother loves her children equally. But maybe just because he's the reincarnation of my original Jazzy, maybe just
because he's Jazzy Junior, it's slightly possible I might perhaps
adore this one barely a half a smidge more than I do Juicy.
Probably not, but possibly yes. I only know when I realized he
suffered from allergies, I got crazy. We noticed his tummy was
chronically upset. His eyes had runny stuff and always needed
to be washed clean. He was forever scratching one ear. These
symptoms never seemed to go away. They weren't critical.
They weren't disabling. But they weren't going away either.

He was tested. Results came back he was highly allergic.
He could not eat chicken or meat or potatoes or beets. We'd
been feeding him lots of chicken and rice because, we
thought, that was always healthy and he loved it. No more
chicken. We could not replace it with bits of beef because
he'd tested positive for that, too. A staple of his diet was a
certain familiar dry dog food pellet, but careful examination
of the ingredients revealed its mixture included beetroot.
Further, he was allergic to grasses and weeds and flowers like
dandelion. We stopped taking him into the country except
to certain homes whose gardens we knew. We had our terrace replanted. We consulted with the vet daily. We consulted with the breeder steadily. We had menus made up by
a holistic specialist in Germany. God, were we busy.

This concept of my being totally consumed with the lone male creature in my life also bothered Alice, my friend the banker. She insisted: "But you must have a man in your life."

"Why?"

"Because you must. You absolutely cannot live singly."

"Look," I said. "Even ecstatic wives are known to offer a prayer of thanks to Our Lady of the Business Trip when they can palm off their guys for two days. It's called a breath of fresh air. Freedom."

"That has nothing to do with what I'm talking about. I'm talking about an emergency. What will you do in an emergency."

"Call 911."

"Not that kind of an emergency. A *real* emergency."

I didn't understand what she was trying to say.

"What does a woman do," she continued, "if she absolutely has to go out and she's in a building with no doorman or elevator man?"

I was still staring at her.

She stepped back to appraise me like I was not very bright. Then she sighed and said slowly: "How can you do up the back of your dress?"

I stopped staring. I had to admit that while Jazzy and Juicy respond to certain words, such as *heel, sit, come, stay,* I had not as yet taught them the command *zip.*

The truth is, with the exception of zipper duties, almost

the only area in which this man of the house and his sister fell seriously short was in terms of fixing things. Both had zero handyman skills. This lack came front and center when Alice shared with me her realization "Every few years it's time for a change. Change your makeup, change your wardrobe, change your favorite restaurants. Change your circle of people. Change your habits. Change your vacation patterns. Change something. You need to clear out, clean out everything. A change needs a *change*."

Since the Adams Family was clearly together until death do us part, all that really needed to be changed was our lifestyle. The conditions at home. My loves were not overnight houseguests. This permanent forever live-in and his sister had to be accommodated. And while I was at it— me, too. In other words, I had to redo our existing living conditions so that my little family and I could go down life's highway together in comfort. That decision fostered a second decision. I needed to fix up my personal john. Mostly because my roommates had decided it was also *their* personal john. Stepping on them was something to which I had become accustomed. Stepping in *it* was not something to which I wished to become accustomed.

The master powder room was smaller than Kate Moss's rear end. My cotenants weren't lobbying for a Jacuzzi and couldn't have cared less about a state-of-the-art glass-enclosed, walk-in steam shower. Nor did they growl about having their very own bidet, since Jazzy appeared content to lift his leg against my leg. But me, I decided to widen my master bath. Simply put, I needed to reconfigure this area just so these loves of my life and I could pee together.

I was excited the morning our project finally began. I could hardly wait until the contractor arrived for his initial assessment. He had called the day before to announce: "I'm bringing with me the boss painter (he pronounced it 'paint-ner'). He's coming from a previous job which, because due to the fact you're such a fine lady and all, we don't want a person such as yourself to be kept waiting. So let's say 11:15. This way you don't waste your time waiting for us."

"Okay, fine," I said. "I'll see you 11:15."

"Sharp."

"Yes, sharp; 11:15 sharp."

"Right. So, see you tomorrow morning 11:15 sharp. If any changes on your part, call me."

"There won't be. See you then."

"Right. Tomorrow we have an 11:15 appointment."

Every morning Juicy wriggled out from under the covers and presented herself on top of my face and neck. She licked my nose, my ears. She waited for me to kiss her nose, her ears in return. We snuggled, we ruffled, we wrestled. And while I read the papers, I massaged Jazzy. He lay on his back, all five legs pointing upward, and I cootchy-cooed his belly. He turned over to get his fur rubbed the wrong way. It was a ritual. Should there be a morning when seconds were precious and I hadn't time, they'd tug at me. This particular day, excited because I was doing all this construction for them, I planned to launch into some extra-special long-time lolling and rolling in the sheets—when the house phone rang.

The contractor was downstairs.

It was 8:00 A.M.

I was in my nightie, which is not a pretty sight. So much cream was schmeared on my face that I nearly slid out of bed. The hairdo I'd slept in had gone south, the mascara I hadn't bothered to remove the night before was now clotted. And my dogs, who hadn't gotten their full complement of ruffling and snuggling, were into their toe fetish phase—licking my feet obsessively. This was not a Kodak moment. I careened around wildly for a robe—and the doorbell rang. To say I thus wasn't presentable and didn't feel in charge of the meeting would have been an understatement.

The Paintner right away discussed what he positively wouldn't do.

One tiny wall papered? "No. This I can't do. Lady, anybody'll tell you that for this you need a union wallpaperer."

"Well, can you paint the air conditioner to match the wall?"

"No. This I can't do. Lady, air conditioners don't get painted, they get sprayed."

"So spray."

"No. This I can't do. Lady, for this you got to hire a metal sprayer."

I indicated a small hole in the baseboard which Juicy had gnawed. "Can you fix that?"

"No. This I can't do. Lady, this requires a master plasterer."

Why the Paintner, who'd obviously taken the Oath of Sadism, couldn't have started this at 11:15, God knows. It became apparent that this Paintner only painted. A Picasso hanging on a nail he'd paint over. He spilled more than I'd ever need for that air conditioner I originally wanted done, and he painted items I didn't want painted—like rugs and windows. With no man of the house other than Jazzy to check his work, whatever was in front of him got daubed. Not removed. Day 2, when some color accidentally splattered on the designated areas, it was considered a bonus.

Day 12—of what was originally assessed to be a three-day job—ushered itself in with overhanging clouds. Dark and gloomy. The man was painting his arm instead of a windowsill. I said, "You can't see anything. Make a light."

He said, "No, this I can't do. Lady, for this you gotta hire an electrician."

That's when relations between him, the Paintner, and me, the Paintnee, became strained. And then I uttered the fearsome phrase "extra coat." Seems the words "extra" and "coat" may be used separately with safety. But never may they be put together in front of a Paintner. You want your black wall white? You get one coat. Request more than one coat and he will blanch, foam, twitch, and lay rigid. At this point nothing but a hypodermic and a half inch of fifties will save him. And, trust me, if you have the half inch of fifties, you can shove that hypodermic.

During this particular mini-crisis, I briefly considered trading my 4½-pound male new Yorkie for a 170-pound male New Yorker. The 170-pounder didn't even have to live in and ask, "So how was it for you?" The hell with foreplay. I needed a foreman.

Take the tile man. I explained: "I want the ceiling off-white."

He gave some sort of eruptive sound. Either a belch from gastritis or a grunt of approval.

"I want it halfway between oyster and eggshell but definitely not yellowy. No creamy tone."

He said nothing, but I could tell he was alive. I saw him breathing. I placed a sample mosaic on a table. Honoring me with a turpentiney burp, he ignored the sample and bellowed to his assistant: "She wants white."

Weeks later his staff of one worker showed. Never did I think glue could be noisy. It wasn't. He was. The ladder fell. He fell. Tools fell. The sink fell. Baghdad wasn't as destroyed. Sympathetic holes began appearing in the tub. As weeks faded into months and summer to winter, I made plans to print napkins saying, "Cindy & The Tile Man."

And that was before the onset of the plumbers. I learned Monday is always a legal holiday for plumbers. Never do they begin a job early in the week so they can finish Friday. If they do that, their shop steward fines them. They always start Thursday, so your house stays wrecked over the weekend while they can lie around their own clean homes.

I was redoing an area the size of a phone booth. What

looked like a three-week, start to finish, job had now consumed my entire home. And life. And time. It was stretch-
ing over months. Ladders, drills, and jackhammers were
housed in my bedroom. The contractor was getting his mail
there.

Juicy's heart-shaped velveteen leopard-skin doggy bed at
my dressing table had to be taken up because that was where
paint cans sat and worktables were set up. Nor could she enter a nook which heretofore had been her personal space
because foreign objects which she could ingest littered the
floor and dust from the demolition which she could lick up
or breathe in was everywhere.

There was the rainy afternoon I had to contain her in a
small area behind a hastily erected doggy gate because there
were tiny tools and nails and shards of concrete scattered all
over. She was not a happy camper. I was bustling about elsewhere, and she desperately wanted out. A few minutes later
the tile man heard banging.

"Who's banging?" he said.

"Nobody," I said. "Nobody else is here."

"There's banging. Somebody's banging. I hear banging."

My smart-ass child had actually stood up on three legs
and with her right front paw pounded repeatedly on that
doggy gate until we took her out.

Jazzy was totally discombobulated. His nighttime water
bowl was usually alongside my sink. Now, because of wet
paint, he couldn't get there. He was so upset that he threw
up on me. Best-selling author Amy Tan, who had years ear-

lier endured that particular unattractive experience on a transatlantic flight, told me she'd learned that the best thing to take away the smell of a dog's whatevers is coffee grounds.

When Nazalene arrived, she sniffed around and said, "You already had coffee? Why? I'm not late."

I said, "I didn't have coffee."

She said, "So who had coffee? There's nobody else here. Jazzy needed coffee?"

I said, "Yes."

She didn't know what I was talking about. She only knew the whole place smelled of Maxwell House.

As Nazalene came in, Jazzy went running, his tail wagging happily, to her side. Once she had petted him, he ran back and whoopsed—right on me—a second time. At eleven o'clock in came Reggie. Jazzy raced up to Reggie. Once Reggie had petted him, he ran back and whoopsed all over me again. This one morning, in the thick and dust of heavy construction, with his bed and water bowl misplaced, with lots of strangers in his own house clumping past him in thick boots paying him no attention, he threw up on me four times.

Not on Reggie. Not on Nazalene. Not on any of the workmen. Not anywhere else in the apartment. Only on me. He was telling me he wasn't happy with me. For months my home smelled like Starbucks.

There was the afternoon I couldn't find them anywhere. They loved the kitchen, which is like a family room. Big overstuffed chairs. Banquette. Hassocks. A cabinet filled with stuffed animals—stuffed bear, stuffed kitty, stuffed dog, stuffed panda. I crawled around that floor searching their favorite corners and nearly ended up with heart failure. No Juicy. No Jazzy. I searched everywhere. I ran inside, outside, I hunted in closets. I was scared beyond belief. Hours later, in panic and frustration, I banged my fists on the cabinet. The cabinet yelped. They'd burrowed into the collection of stuffed toys, and you couldn't tell them from the fakeolas.

Eventually things reached the point where there was little left to paint except where the paint job was beginning to flake off already. The Paintner and I had already exchanged phone numbers preparatory to getting together socially. And came the night the electricians who were installing the bathroom sconces shorted everything out. And I was in the dark with wet paint. And one small area of wet cement. And I was due to entertain Seven.

Seven is not a number in this case. It is a name. It belongs to a six-foot-three-inch black dude with platinum hair and metal spike driven into his lower lip. One of seven, born Marcus Vest in Lexington, Kentucky, the seventh month of 1972, this hip-hop producer for Ja Rule, Eve, Mariah, Whitney, Ashanti, Jay-Z, Tupac, Janet Jackson, Jennifer Lopez, Mary J. Blige, Britney Spears, Alicia Keyes believes seven is numerically mystical, magical, and spiritual.

Since *The Wall Street Journal* called him one of "the next generation of moguls," and since I was still playing Sinatra records, I thought the time had come for me to get with it, so I'd invited him over.

This is a man who is not exactly understated. Embossed black leather pants with salad-plate-size white buttons up the sides. Leather jacket with big 7s on the back and shoulders. Huge white block letters on the front reading, for some reason, "Pre-Crime Division." Bandanna, earrings, multiple rings, double bracelets, gloves with two fingers only, custom boots from the skin of stingrays, and the numeral 7 across his cheek thanks to M.A.C cosmetics.

He launched into stuff like: "J.Lo's ass is phenomenal. It goes out and then it has, like, a balcony in the middle. Distracting as hell."

About Mariah: "I was on guard at first because she has all these security guys around her, but then I went downstairs and it was just her. And she was great."

About Britney: "I'm rejuicing her because she's looking to go street . . . and, hey, if it doesn't work we can always fix it in the mix. I don't usually say, 'Your way sucks.' I just say, 'Let's put both ways up and hear which has the better vibe.'"

Seven had carefully and graciously stepped over the planks in my front hall, bent double under a plastic tunnel the contractor had built thinking it would contain the dust, swiveled to sidestep a dump truck in the living room, and all seventy-five inches of him was now safely wedged into one clean, sterile corner of my library. I was so fascinated eyeing his massive silver right-wrist cuff bracelet with the amethysts and moonstones set in the number 7 and listening to his conversation—"I work hard . . . like twenty hours a day . . . I only sleep on planes and at stoplights . . . music is my mistress"—that I hadn't noticed Jazzy wasn't similarly mesmerized.

He had padded off. With horror I realized that this off he had padded onto was wet cement, because the very instant I noticed he'd padded back was the very instant he leapt onto Seven. Jazzy's paws became permanently inlaid in gray cement on Seven's handmade, custom-tailored, high-class embossed black leather pants. Like those of cosseted and coveted big-time celebrities on the sidewalk outside Grauman's Chinese Theatre in Hollywood, Jazzy's perfect imprint was to remain for time immemorial. Having hardened quickly, the cement was implanted in four places—Seven's right knee, left knee, his crotch—a spectacularly fine specimen right in the groin area. Leather specialists have since declared that these paw prints—like diamonds—are forever.

I didn't really need a husband because I'd lost my rudder, I needed a psychiatrist because what I was losing was my mind.

As J and JJ have taught me, a messy life full of poop and purpose beats nice empty perfection anytime.

Epilogue

I went to the Westminster Dog Show. Forget tall skinny types like Claudia Schiffer and Naomi Campbell. When you're talking major cosmetic improvements strutting a runway, you are talking four-legged models.

Yorkie handlers do serious makeovers. Take one entry in the puppy class. Ditsy was perfect—size, shape, weight, age, hair—she strutted like this was the Chanel catwalk. One problem. Her left ear tip flopped instead of standing straight up. No problem. Her handler fashioned a topknot on which to set a bow and included a few hairs attached to both ears. The taut rubber band that pulled it all into a little pouf snapped that one wiggly ear into position. It then pointed straight up like a reconstructed Pamela Anderson boob.

Another was a prizewinner except he was too silver-blue. He needed to be darker. Rather than lose points because of a minor flaw like his coloring, the handler improved on nature. Yorkies have hair, not fur, so she tinted him with my same shade of L'Oréal. She only had to watch he didn't prance too close to neon. Concentrated artificial backlight made Ryan look purple.

The eyes of Yorkie show dogs are expected to be dark rimmed. That requires eyeliner. The tails of Yorkie show dogs are expected to be up. That means bobby pins at the base of the tail. Teasing and fluffing the backside hair hides the bobbys and does the job. The bodies of Yorkie show dogs are expected to be square. That means (a) making sure the tail stands up, and (b) making sure the topknot is poufed high. Accentuating both ends camouflages a sausagelike dachshund shape. Makes it look boxier. A Yorkie show dog is expected to have certain parts golden blond. That calls for bleach. And that hair is conditioned, lubricated, treated, and greased after every tour jeté in the ring.

The long hanging hair is too curly? Smooth it with a hot curling iron. It's too thin? Too flyaway? Shpritz and hair spray. The floor-length Fu Manchu mustache gets chewed or broken? When eating or playing, it's rubber bands like a ponytail on each side of the mouth.

Some handlers actually resort to cosmetic surgery to improve the bite; some hit dentists to fix the teeth.

Westminster kept replaying in my brain. I couldn't turn it off. I also couldn't sleep. I was dying of heat. I was under layers of tumbled blankets, which are kept deliberately rumply on my bed so the babies can find a pleat or crease or crevice to cuddle into. My quilt and duvet make the surface too smooth. Me, I like cold fresh air. I like sleeping in a crisp frigid room. But Jazzy and Juicy do not like windows wide open. They are not into snow, rain, or brisk temperature. Air-conditioned thermostat-controlled nice Park Avenue indoors is what they like. So, I had to close the windows because Jazzy and Juicy like warm.

With all the blankets piled onto me and no air, I couldn't sleep. Despite it being mid-January, I was sweating. The babies were content—but me, not. As the velvet night closed in and I lay with wide open perspiring eyelids, the Devils again paid me a visit. Not a quiet visit. A rowdy one. They were shouting:

"You're all alone."

"Nobody really cares."

"Suppose you fall . . . suppose you get sick . . ."

"If anything happens, who would know?"

"How long before someone might find you?"

Again it was: Punch the pillow, smooth the sheets, roll over on your side. The Voices get louder:

"Who would you call?"

"Who would rush over?"

"Who would care?"

"Everybody has somebody, you have nobody."

Again it was: Switch on the light, open a book, raid the fridge, switch off the light, crawl back in bed. The Voices:

"You're getting older."

"You need someone with you."

"You shouldn't be alone."

"What if . . ."

The What Ifs began their familiar subdivision. What If there's a fire? What If an earthquake? What If a terrorist attack? What If you can't breathe?

I knew the drill. I knew next up should be the army of Yeah Buts. But I couldn't hear my own thoughts. The Devils were making too much noise in my head. The Voices had become shrill. I thought, No. Not this time. You're not going to win anymore.

Instead of arguing them down, I picked myself up. I got out of bed and did the only intelligent thing. I shuffled into the kitchen. This time no standing in front of the open fridge and inhaling something so stiff and aged and leftover from the third shelf in the back that it was growing penicillin. This time I actually calmed myself. I stole a moment to take a deep breath. I offered up a silent thank-you. I then slowly, deliberately, made myself a fresh tuna on white with Hellmann's mayo. I even toasted the slightly stale white bread. I even sat down at the table to savor each bite.

I thought to myself, Hey, it's okay to be afraid now and then. Everybody's afraid of something at some time. I'm even a little fearful when I dwell on Jazzy Junior's health. He has that list of allergies. But, y'know what? I'm actually okay. I'm content. I'm honestly happy. There's nothing I really want. I just want to keep what I have. I want only for it to continue. I just want more of the same. I love what God has handed me. I love my babies, I love my home, I love the people around me, I love my friends, I love my sandwich, I love what I'm doing. . . . Life is good.